Contents

T5-ARX-638

Introduction

The National Council of Teachers of Mathematics (NCTM) has set specific standards to help students become confident of their mathematical abilities. Communicating mathematically and problem solving are the keys to helping students develop skills to apply in their daily lives and in later careers.

Based on the belief that students learn to reason mathematically in order to become problem-solvers, the strategies in this book show students more than one way to solve problems. These strategies are not absolute techniques, however. Learning a multitude of ways to approach a problem is part of the philosophy in developing sets of problem-solving strategies.

Organization

The chapters offer several strategies to solve a given type of problem: Whole Numbers, Fractions, Improper Fractions and Mixed Numbers, Multiplying Fractions, Dividing Fractions, Decimals, Ratios and Percentages, Probability, Geometry, and Pre-Algebra.

Special Feature

Each chapter concludes with a "Flex Your Math Muscles" activity page that presents an opportunity for students to choose their own strategy to solve problems. These pages provide students with a unique way to approach the challenges. Divergent thinking is promoted in these lessons.

Problem Solving Strategies

The following problem solving strategies are demonstrated:

CHOOSE AN OPERATION   Students determine which operation (addition, subtraction, multiplication, or division) to use based on the information presented.

USE ESTIMATION   Students learn both when and how to estimate answers, based on rounding numbers and performing the appropriate operation. Estimation is encouraged as a strategy in all problem solving to verify reasonableness of answers.

LOOK FOR A PATTERN   This strategy emphasizes pattern recognition of given sequences of numbers, geometric shapes, pictorial information, and other data for problem solving.

GUESS AND CHECK   Students learn a variety of methods to reduce the number of trial and error efforts needed to reach accuracy in answers.

IDENTIFY EXTRA OR MISSING INFORMATION By identifying pertinent information, students learn to recognize information which is extra or missing.

MAKE/USE A DRAWING   Creating visual images of information makes analysis of the facts easier.

USE EQUALITY/INEQUALITY   Students develop strategies to compare fractions for concept development.

MAKE A TABLE   Pattern recognition, identification of extra or missing information, and arrangement of data into a visual form demonstrate the effectiveness of making a table.

USE A GRAPH   Graphing organizes information so that comparisons can be made visually.

IDENTIFY SUBSTEPS   Some complex problems require the completion of more than one step to calculate the solution. This strategy emphasizes the importance of identifying both the given information and the order of operations to reach the solution.

USE LOGICAL REASONING   In this strategy students learn to recognize relationships and to answer the question, "Does it make sense?" Strategies include a process of elimination of answers and visual representation of information to organize the elements of a problem.

WORK BACKWARD   This section introduces a strategy for solving complex problems in which the end result is given. By recognizing clue words and using them to solve the problem, students can work backward from an answer. This skill develops background for later success in algebra.

WRITE A NUMBER SENTENCE Converting written statements into numerical sentences to solve for an unknown is the basis of an algebraic approach. This strategy demonstrates identification of known and unknown information to develop sentences for solutions.

DEFINE MATHEMATICAL TERMS Relating mathematical language and representing symbolism in a variety of ways are extended in problem solving strategies.

Use

This book is designed for independent use by students who have had instruction in the specific skills covered in these lessons. Copies of the activities can be given to individuals, pairs of students, or small groups for completion. They can also be used as a center activity. If students are familiar with the content, the worksheets can be homework for reviewing and reinforcing problem-solving concepts.

To begin, determine the implementation that fits your students' needs and your classroom structure. The following plan suggests a format for this implementation:

1. *Explain* the purpose of the worksheets to your class.
2. *Review* the mechanics of how you want students to work with the exercises.
3. *Review* the specific skill for the students who may not remember the process for successful completion of the computation.
4. *Introduce* students to the process and to the purpose of the activities.
5. *Do* a practice activity together.
6. *Allow* students to experiment, discover, and explore a variety of ways to solve a given problem.

Additional Notes

1. *Bulletin Board.* Display completed worksheets to show student progress.
2. *Center Activities.* Use the worksheets as center activities to give students the opportunity to work cooperatively.

3. *Have fun.* Working with these activities can be fun as well as meaningful for you and your students.

What Research Says

The National Council of Teachers of Mathematics (NCTM) has listed problem solving as a key standard for instructional programs for all students. According to NCTM,

Problem solving is the cornerstone of school mathematics. Without the ability to solve problems, the usefulness and power of mathematical ideas, knowledge, and skills are severely limited. Students who can efficiently and accurately multiply but who cannot identify situations that call for multiplication are not well prepared. Students who can both develop *and* carry out a plan to solve a mathematical problem are exhibiting knowledge that is much deeper and more useful than simply carrying out a computation. Unless students can solve problems, the facts, concepts, and procedures they know are of little use. The goal of school mathematics should be for all students to become increasingly able and willing to engage with and solve problems.

Problem solving is also important because it can serve as a vehicle for learning new mathematical ideas and skills (Schroeder and Lester 1989). A problem-centered approach to teaching mathematics uses interesting and well-selected problems to launch mathematical lessons and engage students. In this way, new ideas, techniques, and mathematical relationships emerge and become the focus of discussion. Good problems can inspire the exploration of important mathematical ideas, nurture persistence, and reinforce the need to understand and use various strategies, mathematical properties, and relationships.

National Council of Teachers of Mathematics. *Principles and Standards for School Mathematics.* Reston, Va.: The National Council of Teachers of Mathematics, 2000.

Schroeder, Thomas L., and Frank K. Lester, Jr. "Developing Understanding in Mathematics via Problem Solving." In *New Directions for Elementary School Mathematics,* 1989 Yearbook of the National Council of Teachers of Mathematics, edited by Paul R. Trafton, pp. 31–42. Reston, Va.: National Council of Teachers of Mathematics, 1989.

Correlation to NCTM Standards

Content Strands	Pages
Number and Operations	
Work flexibly with fractions, decimals, and percents to solve problems	19, 23, 24, 25, 26, 27, 28, 29, 30, 31, 34, 36, 37, 38, 39, 40, 41, 46, 47, 48, 49, 55, 56, 57, 58, 59, 60, 61, 63, 64, 74, 75, 76, 77, 78, 106, 107, 108
Understand and use ratios and proportions to represent quantitative relationships	69, 70, 71, 72, 73, 74
Understand the meaning and effects of arithmetic operations with fractions, decimals, and integers	19, 23, 24, 25, 26, 27, 28, 29, 30, 31, 34, 36, 37, 38, 39, 40, 41, 46, 47, 48, 49, 55, 56, 57, 58, 59, 60, 61, 66, 67, 68, 106, 107, 108
Use the associative and commutative properties of addition and multiplication and the distributive property of multiplication over addition to simplify computations with integers, fractions, and decimals	10, 11, 20, 22, 30, 31, 32, 33, 41, 54, 56, 57, 59, 60, 61, 64, 66, 67, 68, 106, 107, 108
Understand and use the inverse relationships of addition and subtraction, multiplication and division, and squaring and finding the square root to simplify computations and solve problems	18, 30, 32, 33, 41, 54
Select appropriate methods and tools for computing with fractions and decimals from among mental computation, estimation, calculators or computers, and paper and pencil, depending on the situation and apply the selected methods	9, 12, 13, 16, 18, 21, 23, 24, 25, 26, 27, 28, 35, 42, 43, 44, 45, 46, 47, 49, 50, 51, 52, 53, 55, 56, 57, 62, 65, 66, 67, 68
Develop and use strategies to estimate the results of rational-number computations and judge the reasonableness of the results	9
Develop, analyze, and explain methods for solving problems involving proportions, such as scaling and finding equivalent ratios	69, 70, 71, 72, 73, 85, 86, 87, 108

Correlation Chart, page 2

Content Strands	Pages
Algebra	
Develop an initial conceptual understanding of different uses of variables	99, 100, 101, 102, 103, 104, 105
Geometry	
Precisely describe, classify, and understand relationships among types of two- and three-dimensional objects using their defining properties	89, 90, 94
Understand relationships among the angles, side lengths, perimeters, areas, and volume of similar objects	89, 90, 91, 92, 93, 94, 95, 96, 97, 98, 108
Data Analysis and Probability	
Formulate questions, design studies, and collect data about a characteristic shared by two populations or different characteristics within one population	14, 81, 82, 83
Select, create, and use appropriate graphical representations of data, including histograms, box plots, and scatterplots	14, 17, 43, 71, 81
Discuss and understand the correspondence between data sets and their graphical representations, especially histograms, stem-and-leaf plots, box plots, and scatterplots	15
Understand and use appropriate terminology to describe complementary and mutually exclusive events	84, 85, 86, 87
Use proportionality and a basic understanding of probability to make and test conjectures about the results of experiments and simulations	79, 80, 81, 82, 83, 86, 87, 88
Compute probabilities for simple compound events, using such methods as organized lists, tree diagrams, and area models	79, 80, 81, 82, 83, 88
Problem Solving	
Build new mathematical knowledge through problem solving	all
Solve problems that arise in mathematics and in other contexts	all
Apply and adapt a variety of appropriate strategies to solve problems	all
Monitor and reflect on the process of mathematical problem solving	all

Name _____ Date _____

Assessment, page 1

Follow the directions to solve each problem.

Estimate the answer by rounding numbers to the nearest hundreds. The problem may have more than 1 step.

1. Altogether, the rock star's jacket has 3,433 glittery spangles. The collar has 838 spangles. The sleeves have 624 spangles. About how many spangles are on the rest of the jacket? _____

Work backward to solve this problem.

2. Tanya wanted to fill her scrapbook with picture postcards. The scrapbook had 16 pages, and each page held 6 postcards. In 1 town she bought 13 postcards, in another she bought 28 postcards, and in the last town she bought 34 postcards. Did Tanya buy enough postcards to fill her scrapbook? _____

Change the fractions into equivalent fractions to solve this problem.

3. Tyler, Megan, and Janna were in the rope-climbing contest. Tyler climbed $\frac{7}{12}$ of the way up the rope, Megan climbed $\frac{5}{6}$ of the way, and Janna climbed $\frac{2}{3}$ of the way. Who won the contest? _____

Make a plan and choose the correct operations to solve this problem. The problem has more than 1 step.

4. Camela decides to make a pair of pajamas for her dog Fido. She needs $\frac{7}{8}$ of a yard of fabric. She has 1 piece that is $\frac{1}{3}$ of a yard, another piece that is $\frac{1}{4}$ of a yard, and a third piece that is $\frac{5}{12}$ of a yard. Does she have enough fabric to make Fido's pajamas? _____

Write a number sentence to help you solve this problem. Reduce your answer if possible.

5. Each day Thom had to write in the ship log. On the first day he wrote $\frac{3}{4}$ page. On the second day he wrote $\frac{7}{8}$ page. On the third day he wrote $\frac{1}{2}$ page. How many pages did he write altogether? _____

Use guessing and checking to solve this problem.

6. One time Carri was able to drive $6\frac{1}{2}$ laps before she ran out of gas. Today she only went $\frac{2}{3}$ that far before she ran out of gas. How many laps did Carri drive today before she ran out of gas? _____

Name _____ Date _____

Assessment, page 2

Use the graph and logic to help you solve this problem.

7. What fraction of the flour is used to make both the pepperoni and olive pizzas?

_____

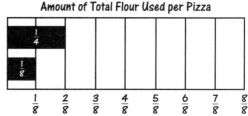

Amount of Total Flour Used per Pizza

Make a drawing to help you solve the problem.

8. For a snack, the 3 baseball players ate $3\frac{3}{4}$ ounces of carrots. If they shared the carrots equally, how many ounces of carrots did each player eat? _____

Cross out the extra facts. Then solve the problem.

9. Greg brought goulash to the party. He used $3\frac{3}{4}$ cups of gravy in his goulash. His recipe makes $10\frac{1}{2}$ large servings. If he divides each serving by $\frac{1}{2}$, how many smaller servings will he have? _____

Solve the problem using a decimal point.

10. The zoo has 1,000 birds in the bird house. The birds eat 675.75 pounds of seed in a week. If each bird eats the same amount, how much seed would 1 bird eat in a week? _____

Choose an operation to solve the problem.

11. Guests at the party drank chocolate milk. Each pitcher held 38 ounces. If 12 guests each drank 9.5 ounces of milk, how many pitchers of milk did they drink? _____

Make a ratio table to help you solve these problems.

12. Ned went to the video arcade. It costs Ned $1.00 to play 2 games. How much would it cost Ned to play 10 games? _____

13. Oranges are on sale at 2 pounds for $0.90. Is this equal to 3 pounds of oranges for $1.35? _____

Problem Solving Strategies 6, SV 0517-0

Assessment, page 3

Use a formula and proportions to help you solve this problem.

14. Stu is 6 feet tall. He is standing by a tree. His shadow is 4 feet long. The tree's shadow is 12 feet long. How tall is the tree? _____

Use the table below to solve this problem. Reduce your answer if possible.

15. Lucy did a survey. She asked her classmates what color backpack they had. She put results in a frequency table. There are 30 students in Lucy's class, so there are 30 possible outcomes.

What is the probability that Shenille has a green or a black backpack?

_____

Color	Number of students
blue	8
red	5
black	4
green	7
gray	6

Write a number sentence to help you solve this problem.

16. Sal had 45 hits in 180 at-bats. What is his batting average? _____

Use a formula to solve this problem. To find the area of a circle, the formula is $A = \pi \times r^2$.

17. A small pizza has a diameter of 8 inches. A large pizza has a diameter of 14 inches. What is the difference in area between the large pizza and the small pizza? _____

Use a formula to solve this problem. To find the volume of a rectangular box, use the formula $V = W \times L \times H$.

18. A square box (cube) has a width of 4 inches. What is the volume of the cube? _____

Write an equation using addition or subtraction for this problem. Then solve the equation. (Hint: Let x = the variable.)

19. Maria has 17 CDs. Of these, 9 are rock music, and the rest are pop music. How many pop music CDs does Maria have? _____

Write an inequality and then solve the problem.

20. Together Nick and Raul scored more than 40 points in a basketball game. Nick scored 6 more points than Raul. How many points might Raul have scored? (Hint: Let x = Raul's score.) _____

Name _____ Date _____

HEAVY METAL LIVES!

Strategy: Use Estimation

You can solve some problems by estimating the answers. An estimate is found by rounding some or all of the numbers, then finding the answer by doing mental math. You can use a calculator to check your answers.

 Read the problem.

Leonita's school sponsored a rock concert. The auditorium has 302 seats. All the seats were sold. The school earned $15.25 on each ticket. About how much money did the school earn?

 Identify the facts.

All 302 seats in the auditorium were sold. The school earned $15.25 for each ticket.

STEP 3 Round all numbers.

302 can be rounded to 300. $15.25 can be rounded to $15.

STEP 4 Estimate the answer.

To find the answer, multiply. Try doing mental math. Think of $15 as $10 + $5. First multiply 300 × $10 = $3,000. Then multiply 300 × $5 = $1,500. To find the total, add $3,000 + $1,500 = $4,500. The school made about $4,500.

Try It!
Estimate the answers by rounding numbers to the nearest hundreds. Some of the problems have more than 1 step.

1. Altogether, the rock star's jacket has 3,433 glittery spangles. The collar has 838 spangles. The sleeves have 624 spangles. About how many spangles are on the rest of the jacket?

_____

2. The concert program has 688 good luck messages. One page holds 92 messages. About how many pages have messages?

_____

3. The band drove to the concert. The first day they drove 339 miles. The second day they drove 278 miles. The third day they drove 215 miles. About how many miles did they drive altogether?

_____

4. If the band returns home by the same route, about how many miles will their total round trip be?

_____

Problem Solving Strategies 6, SV 0517-0

Name _____ Date _____

GET READY!

Strategy: Choose an Operation

Sometimes a problem does not tell you to add, subtract, multiply, or divide. Read the problem carefully to choose the correct operation.

STEP 1 ▸ **Read the problem.**
Mr. Rigman's class is having a party. If each of the 33 students sells 1 ticket for $6, how much money will the class collect?

STEP 2 ▸ **Identify the facts.**
There are 33 students in the class. Each student will sell 1 ticket. Tickets cost $6 each.

STEP 3 ▸ **Choose an operation.**
Although you could add $6 (price of ticket) 33 (number of students) times, it is faster to multiply.

STEP 4 ▸ **Multiply. Solve the problem.**
$6 a ticket × 33 students = $198
The class will collect $198 from ticket sales.

Try It! Choose an operation to solve each problem.

1. Angela ordered 429 decorations for the party. If the 33 students in her class share equally, how many decorations will each student get?

_____

2. Other students could trade in 16 soup labels for 1 free ticket to the party. If the class collected 832 soup labels, how many free tickets did they give away?

_____

3. The students made popcorn for the party. Each cup of unpopped popcorn held 228 kernels. They used 142 cups of popcorn. How many kernels of unpopped popcorn did they use?

_____

4. After the party students made donations of gloves and mittens to the needy. If 135 students gave 1,215 pairs of gloves and mittens, how many pairs did each student donate?

_____

Problem Solving Strategies 6, SV 0517-0

Name _____ Date _____

ON A WHIRLWIND TOUR!

Strategy: Identify Substeps

Some problems use more than 1 operation. You may have to add, subtract, multiply, and divide in any order.

STEP 1 **Read the problem.**

Raul plans to meet his penpals while on tour with the orchestra. Geoffrey, his English penpal, lives 120 kilometers from London. Raul will drive halfway to meet Geoffrey. He will travel at 30 kph. How long will it take Raul to make the round trip from London?

STEP 2 **Identify the substeps.**

Substep 1: To find how many kilometers is halfway, divide.

Substep 2: To find how long it will take Raul to travel that distance, divide.

Substep 3: To find how long it will take Raul to make the round trip, multiply.

STEP 3 **Work the substeps. Solve the problem.**

Substep 1: $\frac{1}{2}$ of 120 kilometers = $120 \div 2 = 60$ km

Substep 2: 60 km $\div$ 30 kph = 2 hours

Substep 3: 2 hours each way $\times$ 2 ways = 4 hours for the round trip

It will take Raul 4 hours to make the round trip.

Try It! Identify the substeps to solve each problem.

1. Raul will meet his penpal Hans in Hamburg, Germany. Then he will travel 480 km to rejoin the orchestra. He will leave Hamburg at 8 A.M. and travel 80 kph to be at the next theater by 3 P.M. How much time will the trip take Raul?

_____

2. Will he get to the theater on time?

_____

3. Raul had $300 to spend on his trip. He bought a train ticket in England for $48 and a train ticket in Germany for $160. His other expenses amounted to $73. At his last stop he found a souvenir he wanted to buy for $24. Did he have enough money to buy the souvenir?

_____

4. How much money did Raul have left?

_____

Name _____ Date _____

WHAT'S YOUR GUESS?

Strategy: Guess and Check

One fast way to solve problems is to guess the answer, then check it. If your guess is not right, try again. Use what you learn from the first guess to make your next guess better. Guess and check until you find the right answer.

 STEP 1 **Read the problem.**
What operations will complete this problem correctly? Write $\times$ or $\div$ on the lines to complete the problem. Use a calculator to check your answers.

1,896 _____ 79 _____ 2 = 48

STEP 2 **Guess and check. Solve the problem.**
Guess: 48 is smaller than 1,896, so divide first.
Check: $1,896 \div 79 = 24$
Guess: 48 is larger than 24, so multiply next.
Check: $24 \times 2 = 48$
Check again: $1,896 \div 79 \times 2 = 48$

Try It!
Guess and check to solve the problems. Work from left to right. Use a calculator to help you solve each problem.

1. Robyn won tickets to the amusement park by solving this puzzle. She had to multiply and divide to find the answer. Can you solve the puzzle?

   675 _____ 33 _____ 75 = 297

2. Fred won 2 tickets to the ball game by working this puzzle. He had to add, subtract, and multiply to get the right answer. Can you work the problem?

   210 _____ 3 _____ 321 _____ 4 = 313

3. If Jeff can solve this problem, he will win a free movie ticket. He knows he must add, subtract, multiply, and divide to find the answer. Help him find the correct order.

   195 _____ 3 _____ 4 _____ 24 _____ 5 = 28

Name _____ Date _____

TOURING THE SOUTHWEST

Strategy: Work Backward

Sometimes all the information you need is not at the beginning of a problem. It is helpful to work backward to solve such problems. Read the problem carefully. Then work backward to find the answer.

 STEP 1 **Read the problem.**

Tanya is taking a tour of the Southwest. If she writes a 15-page report about the trip, she will earn extra credit in social studies. So far she has written 148 sentences about Mexican history, 136 sentences about American history, and 128 sentences about the desert. If 30 sentences equal 1 page, how many more sentences must Tanya write to complete her report?

STEP 2 **Make a list of what you need to know.**

To find the number of sentences Tanya has already written, add.
To find the numbers of sentences needed altogether, multiply.
To find the number of sentences Tanya still has to write, subtract.

STEP 3 **Work backward. Solve the problem.**

148 + 136 + 128 = 412 sentences written
30 sentences per page × 15 pages = 450 total sentences needed
450 sentences needed − 412 sentences written = 38
Tanya still needs to write 38 sentences to complete her report.

Try It! Work backward to solve these problems.

1. Tanya learned that long ago 11,045 Native Americans had lived in 47 villages. The same number of people lived in each village. Then all but 16 villages vanished. How many people were in the villages that vanished?

_____

2. How many people were in the villages that remained?

_____

3. Tanya wanted to fill her scrapbook with picture postcards. The scrapbook had 16 pages, and each page held 6 postcards. In 1 town she bought 13 postcards, in another she bought 28 postcards, and in the last town she bought 34 postcards. Did Tanya buy enough postcards to fill her scrapbook?

_____

4. How many more postcards did she need?

_____

Name _____ Date _____

ON THE ROAD AGAIN!

Strategy: Use a Graph

A graph is a special table of facts. A pictograph shows information with pictures. To read a pictograph, find the key to see how much each picture or symbol represents.

Notice the numbers at the top of the graph below. Then notice the words at the top: Number of Tickets Sold. These words tell you what information the graph contains. The key tells you that each ticket symbol represents 1,000. You should multiply the numbers at the top of the graph by 1,000. So, for example, in Tampa 40,000 tickets were sold.

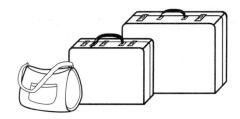

Number of Tickets Sold

	10	20	30	40	50	60	70	80
Anaheim, CA	🎫	🎫	🎫	🎫	🎫	🎫	🎫	
Tampa, FL	🎫	🎫	🎫	🎫				
Cleveland, OH	🎫	🎫	🎫	🎫	🎫	🎫		

Cities

Key: 🎫 = 1,000

STEP 1 ▷ Read the problem.
The agent for the rock group Delta wants to know which city had their largest crowd on their last tour. She will include the city again in their next tour. She is considering Anaheim, Tampa, and Cleveland. Which city should she choose?

STEP 2 ▷ Read the graph.
Find the city name. Then move your finger across the graph to where the pictures end. Then move your finger to the top of the graph to find the number of tickets sold, in thousands.

STEP 3 ▷ Write the facts.
The graph shows that 70,000 tickets were sold in Anaheim; 40,000 tickets were sold in Tampa; and 60,000 tickets were sold in Cleveland.

STEP 4 ▷ Solve the problem.
The graph shows that Delta's largest crowd was in Anaheim, so the agent should schedule that city for the next tour.

Name _____ Date _____

ON THE ROAD AGAIN! part 2

Strategy: Use a Graph

A bar graph contains information in the shape of bars. The length of a bar represents a number. To read a bar graph, match the bars with the numbers.

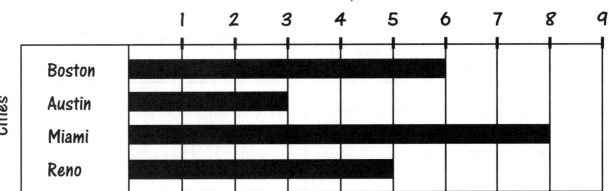

Shirt Sales, in thousands

Cities		
Boston	6	
Austin	3	
Miami	8	
Reno	5	

Try It! Solve these problems using the graph.

1. The rock group Sharks sells T-shirts at each concert. In which city did they sell the most T-shirts?

_____

2. In which city did they sell the fewest T-shirts?

_____

3. How many T-shirts did they sell altogether in Boston and Reno?

_____

4. How many T-shirts did they sell altogether in the 4 cities?

_____

5. If their T-shirts sell for $11 each, how much money did they earn in Austin?

_____

6. How much did they earn in Boston?

_____

7. How much did they earn altogether?

_____

Problem Solving Strategies 6, SV 0517-0

Name _____ Date _____

Unit 1 Review

Strategies
- Use Estimation
- Choose an Operation
- Identify Substeps
- Work Backward

Show What You Know!

Solve each problem. Identify the strategy you used.

1. Kate bought a bedroom set for $2,250. If she pays for it with 25 equal monthly payments, how much will each monthly payment be?

_____

2. Jerry will win 3 CDs if he can solve this problem. He has to subtract, multiply, and divide. Can you work the problem?

224 _____ 2 _____ 12 _____ 3 = 300

3. Lisa gave 10 sheets of graph paper to Ted and 8 sheets to Nancy. Then Jill gave Lisa 12 sheets of graph paper. Lisa now has 35 sheets. How many sheets did she have to begin with?

_____

4. Bruce has earned $87. To buy a new stereo, he needs twice that amount, plus $50. How much does the stereo cost?

_____

5. Mrs. Reyna's class collected cans for recycling. Mike collected 129 cans, Bill collected 82 cans, and Sharim collected 247 cans. About how many cans were collected by the 3 students?

_____

Name _____ Date _____

Unit 1 Review, page 2

Strategy: Use a Graph

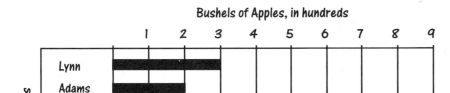

Bushels of Apples, in hundreds

Orchards: Lynn, Adams, Smith, Hirota, Tussi

Apples

Show What You Know!   Use the graph to solve the problems.

1. The Good Apple Company owns 5 apple orchards. Which orchard produced the most apples?

_____

2. Which orchard produced the fewest apples?

_____

3. How many apples did the Smith and Tussi orchards produce altogether?

_____

4. How many apples did all 5 orchards produce?

_____

5. If a bushel of apples sells for $5, how much money did the company earn from the Adams Orchard?

_____

6. How much did it earn from the Lynn Orchard?

_____

7. How much did it earn from all the orchards?

_____

Extension..

What is the most popular weekend retreat in your state? Take a survey. Ask 20 people to say where they would most like to go for a weekend trip. Make a chart that shows the information that you collected and evaluate the results of the survey. What can you conclude?

Problem Solving Strategies 6, SV 0517-0

Name _____ Date _____

You are a real math magician when you can work complicated problems in your head. Can you work this one in your head?

$$5 \times 32 \times 744 \times 6{,}543 \times 0 \times 91 \times 65 = \underline{\qquad}$$

You can also use a calculator to check your answer. Work from left to right. Which way is easier to solve the problem, using your head or using a calculator?

Here is a game of 2s. Put in the right operation signs to make each problem work.

a.	2	2	2	2	=	1	_____
b.	2	2	2	2	=	2	_____
c.	2	2	2	2	=	3	_____
d.	2	2	2	2	=	4	_____
e.	2	2	2	2	=	5	_____
f.	2	2	2	2	=	6	_____

Now try it with 3s.

a.	3	3	3	3	=	3	_____
b.	3	3	3	3	=	4	_____
c.	3	3	3	3	=	5	_____
d.	3	3	3	3	=	6	_____
e.	3	3	3	3	=	7	_____

Name _____ Date _____

FRACTIONS DEPARTMENT STORE

Strategy: Make a Drawing

When solving problems, you sometimes need to work with parts of a whole or parts of a group. Fractions are equal parts of a whole. A drawing can help to show the parts.

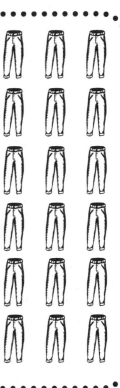

STEP 1 ▷ Read the problem.

The jeans racks at the store are divided into 3 equal sections. Each section is $\frac{1}{3}$ of all the racks. Carmen has 18 pairs of jeans to put on the racks. If she divides the jeans equally among the 3 sections, how many jeans will be in each section?

STEP 2 ▷ Identify the facts.

There are 3 equal sections. There are 18 pairs of jeans. Carmen divides the jeans equally among the 3 sections.

STEP 3 ▷ Make a drawing. Solve the problem.

Separate the jeans into 3 equal groups. Draw a circle around $\frac{1}{3}$ of the jeans in the drawing above.

18 pairs ÷ 3 = 6

Each section holds 6 pairs, or $\frac{1}{3}$ of all the jeans.

Try It! Make a drawing to help you solve the problems.

1. Carmen has 4 shelves for shirts. She has 16 shirts to put on the shelves. If she divides the shirts equally among the 4 shelves, how many shirts will she put on each shelf?

   _____

2. What fraction of the shirts will she put on each shelf?

   _____

3. A rich customer buys 10 dresses at the store. She wants Carmen to send an equal number of the dresses to each of 5 friends. How many dresses will Carmen send to each friend?

   _____

4. What fraction of the dresses will each friend receive?

   _____

Name _____ Date _____

BIG TOY SALE!

Strategy: Choose an Operation

Sometimes a problem does not tell you to add or subtract. Then you must decide which operation to choose to solve the problem.

STEP 1 ▷ Read the problem.
During the big sale, toys with red tags are $3.00 off and toys with green tags are $2.00 off. Larry put red tags on $\frac{3}{8}$ of all the toys, and he put green tags on $\frac{1}{8}$ of all the toys. Altogether, what fraction of all the toys are tagged for the sale?

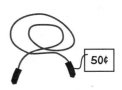
50¢

STEP 2 ▷ Choose an operation.
Look for key words to help you decide which operation to use. *Altogether* signals addition. To find what fraction of the toys are tagged, you must add.

35¢

STEP 3 ▷ Add. Solve the problem.
When adding or subtracting fractions with like denominators, add the numerators. Keep the denominators the same. Reduce your answer if possible.

$\frac{3}{8} + \frac{1}{8} = \frac{4}{8} = \frac{1}{2}$ $\frac{1}{2}$ of all the toys are tagged.

Try It!   Choose an operation to solve each problem.

1. Edwin went to the big toy sale. He noticed that $\frac{5}{6}$ of the dinosaur toys were on sale, but only $\frac{4}{6}$ of the shark toys were on sale. What fraction more of the dinosaur toys were on sale?

_____

2. Edwin decided to buy some party favors. Of his total purchase, $\frac{1}{7}$ were whistles, $\frac{2}{7}$ were tops, and the rest were yo-yos. What fraction of his purchase were yo-yos?

_____

3. Nora went to the sale, too. She noticed that $\frac{5}{12}$ of the dolls were blonde and $\frac{3}{12}$ of the dolls were brunette. What fraction of the dolls were blonde or brunette?

_____

4. What fraction of the dolls were not blonde or brunette?

_____

Name _____ Date _____

READY, SET, GO!

Strategy: Use Equivalent Fractions

Sometimes you must work with fractions that do not have like denominators. Then you must change them into equivalent fractions by reducing them or changing them to higher terms.

STEP 1 **Read the problem.**

One day the gym teacher held a contest. She wanted to see who could climb higher up a rope. The first 2 climbers were Max and Casey. Max climbed $\frac{3}{4}$ of the way up the rope. Casey climbed $\frac{5}{8}$ of the way. Who won the contest?

STEP 2 **Change the fractions to equivalent fractions.**

Compare the denominators. 8 is a multiple of 4. So $\frac{3}{4}$ can be changed to $\frac{6}{8}$ by multiplying the numerator and the denominator by 2.

STEP 3 **Compare the fractions. Solve the problem.**

$\frac{3}{4} = \frac{6}{8}$ $\frac{6}{8}$ is greater than $\frac{5}{8}$. So Max won the contest.

Try It! Change the fractions into equivalent fractions to solve these problems.

1. Tyler, Megan, and Janna were also in the rope-climbing contest. Tyler climbed $\frac{7}{12}$ of the way up the rope, Megan climbed $\frac{5}{6}$ of the way, and Janna climbed $\frac{2}{3}$ of the way. Who won this time?

_____

2. Another part of the contest was the running race. Jimmy ran $\frac{4}{5}$ of a mile, Jarrett ran $\frac{13}{20}$ of a mile, and Jennifer ran $\frac{7}{10}$ of a mile. Who ran the farthest?

_____

3. There was also a free-throw contest. Each person had 24 shots. Val hit $\frac{7}{8}$ of his shots, Mary hit $\frac{11}{12}$ of her shots, and Bobby hit $\frac{3}{4}$ of his shots. Who won the free-throw contest?

_____

4. In the last contest, students stood on their heads as long as they could. Katie stood on her head for $\frac{1}{2}$ a minute, Carl stood on his for $\frac{7}{15}$ of a minute, and Charlene stood on her head for $\frac{3}{10}$ of a minute. Who won this contest?

_____

Name _____ Date _____

WRAP IT UP!

Strategy: Choose an Operation

Sometimes a problem will not tell you to add or subtract. Then you must decide which operation to use to solve the problem.

STEP 1 Read the problem.
Fractions Department Store wraps gifts for customers. On 1 gift Angie used $\frac{3}{5}$ of a roll of ribbon. On another gift she used $\frac{6}{25}$ of a roll of ribbon. What fraction of the roll of ribbon did she use altogether?

STEP 2 Choose an operation.
Look for key words to help you decide which operation to use. *Altogether* signals addition. To find the total amount of ribbon used, add.

STEP 3 Add. Solve the problem.
First you must change the fractions into equivalent fractions. Then add. Reduce the answer if possible.

$$\frac{3}{5} + \frac{6}{25} = \frac{15}{25} + \frac{6}{25} = \frac{21}{25}$$ Angie used $\frac{21}{25}$ of the roll of ribbon.

Try It! Choose an operation to solve each problem. Reduce your answers if possible.

1. Angie sorted the gift box tops and bottoms. She found $\frac{9}{16}$ of the tops and $\frac{5}{8}$ of the bottoms. Did she find more tops or bottoms?

   _____

2. One day Angie wrapped a big box. She used $\frac{2}{3}$ of a roll of paper to wrap the sides and $\frac{2}{9}$ to wrap the rest of the box. What fraction of a roll of paper did Angie use to wrap the box?

   _____

3. What fraction of the roll of paper was left?

   _____

4. On Thursday Angie used $\frac{1}{8}$ of all the bows to wrap gifts. On Friday she used $\frac{1}{2}$ of all the bows. What fraction of all the bows did Angie use?

   _____

5. What fraction of all the bows were left?

   _____

6. Angie used silver ribbon on $\frac{4}{7}$ of all the gifts she wrapped. She used gold ribbon on all the rest. What fraction of the gifts had gold ribbon?

   _____

Problem Solving Strategies 6, SV 0517-0

Name _____ Date _____

A BED FOR FIDO

Strategy: Identify Substeps

Sometimes to solve a problem you must use more than 1 operation. You must decide which operations to use and in what order they must be used.

STEP 1 ▶ **Read the problem.**
Camela is going to build a bed for Fido. She needs $\frac{3}{4}$ of a sheet of plywood to build the bed. She found 1 piece that was $\frac{3}{12}$ of a sheet and another that was $\frac{3}{9}$ of a sheet. Does she have enough plywood with these 2 pieces?

STEP 2 ▶ **Identify the substeps.**
Substep 1: To find how much plywood Camela has, add.
Substep 2: To find if she has enough plywood, compare what she has to what she needs.

STEP 3 ▶ **Work the substeps. Solve the problem.**
Remember to change the fractions into equivalent fractions.

$\frac{3}{12} + \frac{3}{9} = \frac{9}{36} + \frac{12}{36} = \frac{21}{36} = \frac{7}{12}$ is the wood she has.

Then compare the fractions to see if she has enough.

$\frac{3}{4}$ is the wood she needs $= \frac{9}{12}$ $\qquad$ $\frac{7}{12}$ is the wood she has $\qquad$ $\frac{7}{12} < \frac{9}{12}$

Camela does not have enough wood to build Fido's bed.

Try It! Identify the substeps and choose operations to solve each problem.

1. If Camela has $\frac{7}{12}$ of a sheet of plywood and she needs $\frac{3}{4}$ of a sheet to build Fido's bed, how much more plywood does she need?

_____

2. Camela decides to make a pair of pajamas for poor Fido. She needs $\frac{7}{8}$ of a yard of fabric. She has 1 piece that is $\frac{1}{3}$ of a yard, another piece that is $\frac{1}{4}$ of a yard, and a third piece that is $\frac{5}{12}$ of a yard. Does she have enough fabric to make Fido's pajamas?

_____

3. On Monday Fido ate $\frac{3}{4}$ of a bag of food. On Tuesday he ate $\frac{1}{6}$ of a bag. What fraction of the bag of food did Fido eat on the 2 days?

_____

4. What fraction of the bag of food does Fido have left?

_____

WOODSHOP WORK

Strategy: Identify Substeps

Sometimes to solve a problem you must use more than 1 operation. You must decide which operations to use and in what order they must be used.

STEP 1 ▷ Read the problem.

Fran is building display counters. She will use 110 feet of wood to make 5 counters. With 30 feet of wood, she has made a 10-foot counter. With 24 feet of wood she has made an 8-foot counter, and 16 feet of wood made a 4-foot counter. To use all the 110 feet of wood, what are the sizes of the last 2 counters?

STEP 2 ▷ Identify the facts.

Fact 1: *Fran will use 110 feet of wood.*

Fact 2: *30 feet or $\frac{30}{110}$ of the wood made a 10-foot counter.*

Fact 3: *24 feet or $\frac{24}{110}$ of the wood made an 8-foot counter.*

Fact 4: *16 feet or $\frac{16}{110}$ of the wood made a 4-foot counter.*

Fact 5: *Fran will make 5 counters.*

STEP 3 ▷ Identify the substeps.

Substep 1: To find how much wood has already been used, add.
Substep 2: To find how much more wood she has, subtract.
Substep 3: To find the sizes of the last 2 counters, use guess and check.

STEP 4 ▷ Work the substeps. Solve the problem.

Substep 1: $\frac{30}{110} + \frac{24}{110} + \frac{16}{110} = \frac{70}{110}$

Substep 2: $\frac{110}{110} - \frac{70}{110} = \frac{40}{110}$

She has 40 feet of wood, or $\frac{40}{110}$, left to make 2 counters.

Substep 3: $\frac{40}{110} = \frac{24}{110} + \frac{16}{110}$

The last 2 sizes will be an 8-foot counter and a 4-foot counter.

Name _____ Date _____

WOODSHOP WORK, part 2

Strategy: Identify Substeps

```
30 feet of wood  =  10-foot counter
24 feet of wood  =   8-foot counter
16 feet of wood  =   4-foot counter
```

Try It! Use the table and identify the substeps to solve the problems.

1. Fran made another display. She used a total of 132 feet of wood. She made a 10-foot counter, an 8-foot counter, and 2 of the 4-foot counters. She had to make 2 more counters in different sizes. How many feet of wood did she use for the last 2 counters?

_____

2. What size counters could she make?

_____

3. Chuck also made a display. He made 3 of the 10-foot counters, 2 of the 8-foot counters, and a 4-foot counter. How many total feet of counters did he build?

_____

4. What fraction of the total were the 10-foot counters?

_____

5. What fraction of the total were the 8-foot counters?

_____

6. What fraction of the total was the 4-foot counter?

_____

7. Chuck had 64 feet of wood left over from his earlier project. He had to make at least 2 different sizes of counters. What sizes and how many of each could he make with the leftover wood?

_____

8. What fraction of the total amount of wood would each size be?

_____

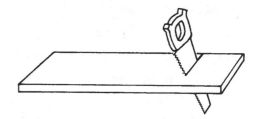

Name _____ Date _____

Unit 2 Review

Show What You Know!

Solve each problem. Reduce your answer if possible. Identify the strategy you used.

1. Liz bought a new photograph album with 10 pages. She can fit 4 photographs on each page. If she fills the entire album, what fraction of photographs will go on each page? Make a drawing to help you solve the problem.

_____

2. Yuki compared his rock collection to Samuel's. Yuki noted that $\frac{6}{12}$ of his collection were igneous rocks. Samuel said that $\frac{1}{3}$ of his rocks were igneous. Who had more igneous rocks?

_____

3. Tomás worked for $\frac{2}{4}$ hour doing math homework and $\frac{3}{4}$ hour doing science homework. How much time did Tomás spend doing homework?

_____

4. Abigail made bracelets for her friends. Each bracelet has $\frac{2}{7}$ blue beads and $\frac{3}{5}$ green beads. The rest of the beads are red. What fraction of the beads are red?

_____

5. The coach kept basketballs, volleyballs, and footballs in a large container. When the coach did an inventory, he jotted down that $\frac{3}{10}$ of the balls were basketballs and $\frac{3}{10}$ were volleyballs. What fraction of the balls were basketballs and volleyballs?

_____

Problem Solving Strategies 6, SV 0517-0

Unit 2 Review, page 2

Strategy: Use a Table

> 4 yards = small costume
>
> 7 yards = medium costume
>
> 10 yards = large costume

Show What You Know!

Use the table to solve the problems.

1. The drama teacher made costumes for the school play. She made 3 small costumes, 5 medium costumes, and 2 large costumes. What fraction of the costumes were small?

_____

2. What fraction represents the number of large and small costumes altogether?

_____

3. The drama teacher bought 70 yards of material. What fraction of the material did she use for the medium costumes?

_____

4. What fraction of the material did she use for all the costumes?

_____

5. What fraction of the material did she have left after making all the costumes?

_____

6. Could the drama teacher make another costume with the leftover material? Explain your answer.

_____

Extension

Look at the hair color of the students in one of your classes. What fraction tells how many students have brown hair? What fraction tells how many students have black hair? What fraction tells how many students have blonde hair? What fraction tells how many students have red hair? What can you conclude about the hair color of the students in the class?

Name _____ Date _____

Flex loves to have fun in his spare time. Solve these problems about Flex's fun activities.

1

If Flex eats all but $\frac{1}{4}$ of a pie, how much pie does he have left?

_____

2

Flex has a really big watermelon. He gives $\frac{1}{2}$ to Jim and $\frac{1}{2}$ to Jane. How much watermelon does he have left for himself?

_____

3

Flex won $20,000 in a contest. He decided to keep $\frac{1}{2}$ for himself. He gave $\frac{3}{10}$ to his brother and $\frac{1}{5}$ to his sister. How much money did each person get?

_____

4

Using the money he won, Flex took his woodworking club of 24 people to the fun park. There $\frac{3}{8}$ of the people rode the roller coaster, $\frac{1}{4}$ rode the bumper cars, and $\frac{5}{24}$ rode the water ride. Only $\frac{1}{6}$ went to the funhouse. Did all of the people in Flex's club do an activity?

_____

5

Flex needs $\frac{10}{12}$ of a yard of fabric to sew a shirt. He can buy $\frac{5}{6}$ of a yard of fabric for $4.50 or $\frac{3}{4}$ of a yard of fabric for $4.00. Which fabric should he buy to make his shirt?

_____

Name _____ Date _____

LOST IN SPACE!

Strategy: Make a Model

A proper fraction is one whose numerator is smaller than its denominator. Examples of proper fractions are $\frac{1}{2}$ or $\frac{3}{4}$. Equivalent fractions are fractions that have the same value, though they have different numerators and denominators. For example, $\frac{1}{3}$ and $\frac{2}{6}$ are equivalent fractions. A drawing can often help you to solve problems about fractions more easily.

STEP 1 **Read the problem.**

Tanisha and Dara were on a secret space mission. But their spaceship was knocked off course by an asteroid. Dara feared they were out of radio range. One radio signal went $\frac{1}{2}$ of the way back to the base. A second signal went $\frac{2}{4}$ of the way, and a third signal went $\frac{3}{6}$ of the way. Did any of the signals reach base?

STEP 2 **Make a model.**

You can answer the question by drawing 3 models to show how far each signal traveled.

You can see that $\frac{1}{2} = \frac{2}{4} = \frac{3}{6}$. None of the signals reached base.

Try It! Make a model to help you solve each problem.

1. When the asteroid hit the spaceship, it damaged the antennas. After the collision, $\frac{3}{4}$ of the radio antenna was left, and $\frac{9}{12}$ of the telescope antenna remained. Which antenna had more remaining?

   _____

2. Tanisha and Dara were lost in space. On Monday they used $\frac{3}{10}$ tank of fuel. On Tuesday they used $\frac{2}{5}$ tank of fuel. On which day did they use more fuel?

   _____

3. Because they were lost, Tanisha worried $\frac{1}{3}$ of the time and Dara worried $\frac{3}{9}$ of the time. Who worried more?

   _____

4. On Wednesday Dara spent $\frac{3}{10}$ of her time sending radio signals. Tanisha spent $\frac{3}{5}$ of her time sending signals. Who spent more time sending radio signals?

   _____

Unit 3, Improper Fractions and Mixed Numbers
Problem Solving Strategies 6, SV 0517-0

Name _____ Date _____

WILL WE SURVIVE?

Strategy: Identify Substeps

Sometimes solving a problem means using more than 1 operation.

An improper fraction is one whose numerator is greater than or equal to its denominator. Both $\frac{6}{6}$ and $\frac{7}{6}$ are improper fractions. To change improper fractions into mixed numbers, first divide the numerator by the denominator. If there is a remainder, write the remainder over the denominator.

$\frac{6}{6}$ (improper fraction) $= 6 \div 6 = 1$ (whole number)

$\frac{7}{6}$ (improper fraction) $= 7 \div 6 = 1$ R1 $= 1\frac{1}{6}$ (mixed number)

STEP 1 ▷ **Read the problem.**

On Thursday Dara checked their food supply. One storage locker held $\frac{32}{10}$ pounds of food. Another locker held $\frac{28}{10}$ pounds, and a third held $\frac{40}{10}$ pounds. If they share the food equally, how many pounds do Tanisha and Dara each have left?

STEP 2 ▷ **Identify the substeps.**

Substep 1: Add the amounts of food in the 3 storage lockers.
Substep 2: Change the improper fractions into mixed or whole numbers.
Substep 3: Divide the total amount of food remaining by 2.

STEP 3 ▷ **Work the substeps. Solve the problem.**

Reduce answers if possible.

$\frac{32}{10} + \frac{28}{10} + \frac{40}{10} = \frac{100}{10}$ pounds of food remaining

$\frac{100}{10} = 10$ pounds $\div 2 = 5$ pounds

Tanisha and Dara each have 5 pounds of food left.

Try It! Identify the substeps to solve each problem.

1. Tanisha checked the oxygen supply. One canister held $\frac{9}{5}$ units, a second held $\frac{13}{5}$ units, and a third held $\frac{6}{5}$ units. If together Tanisha and Dara used $\frac{10}{5}$ units of oxygen a day, did they have enough oxygen for 3 days?

_____

2. Tanisha also checked the fuel supply. One tank held $\frac{8}{4}$ liters, another held $\frac{14}{4}$ liters, and a third held $\frac{11}{4}$ liters. How much fuel did they have left?

_____

Name _____ Date _____

WHERE ARE WE?

Strategy: Write a Number Sentence

To add or subtract fractions, it is often easier to have fractions with like denominators. So you might need to change one or more of the fractions into equivalent fractions. To reduce, or simplify, a fraction, you must find the smallest equivalent fraction. To find the smallest equivalent, divide the numerator and denominator by the greatest possible number. To change the fraction to an equivalent fraction in higher terms, multiply the numerator and denominator by the same number. To change an improper fraction to a mixed number, divide the numerator by the denominator.

STEP 1 **Read the problem.**

On the first day after the collision, the spaceship traveled $\frac{3}{4}$ light-year. On the second day it traveled $\frac{2}{3}$ light-year. How far did the spaceship travel on the 2 days?

STEP 2 **Write a number sentence.**

$\frac{3}{4}$ light-year $+ \frac{2}{3}$ light-year $=$ total distance traveled

STEP 3 **Add. Solve the problem.**

Since $\frac{3}{4}$ and $\frac{2}{3}$ cannot be reduced, you must change them into equivalent fractions in higher terms. Be sure to change the improper fraction.

$$\frac{3}{4} = \frac{9}{12} \qquad \frac{2}{3} = \frac{8}{12} \qquad \frac{9}{12} + \frac{8}{12} = \frac{17}{12} = 1\frac{5}{12}$$

The spaceship traveled $1\frac{5}{12}$ light-years on the 2 days.

 Try It! Write a number sentence to help you solve each problem. Reduce your answers if possible.

1. Each day Tanisha had to write in the ship log. On the first day she wrote $\frac{3}{4}$ page. On the second day she wrote $\frac{7}{8}$ page. On the third day she wrote $\frac{1}{2}$ page. On which day did she write the most?

_____

2. How many pages did she write altogether?

_____

3. Dara finally located 2 nearby planets. Planet K was $\frac{2}{3}$ light-year away. Planet Z was $\frac{3}{5}$ light-year away. Which planet was closer?

_____

4. What was the difference in distance between the 2 planets?

_____

Unit 3, Improper Fractions and Mixed Numbers
Problem Solving Strategies 6, SV 0517-0

Name _____ Date _____

PLANET, YO!

Strategy: Choose an Operation

Sometimes a problem does not tell you to add or subtract. You must read the problem carefully to choose the correct operation.

 Read the problem.

Dara and Tanisha decided to go to Planet Z. On the first day they traveled $1\frac{1}{5}$ light-years. On the second day they traveled $1\frac{3}{10}$ light-years. How far did they travel altogether?

 Choose an operation.

Look for key words to help you decide which operation to use. *Altogether* signals addition. To find how far they traveled, add.

STEP 3 **Add. Solve the problem.**

To add, you must have fractions with like denominators. First change the fractions into equivalent fractions. $\frac{1}{5} = \frac{2}{10}$. $\frac{3}{10}$ does not need to be changed. Reduce the answer if possible.

$1\frac{2}{10} + 1\frac{3}{10} = 2\frac{5}{10} = 2\frac{1}{2}$

They traveled $2\frac{1}{2}$ light-years altogether.

Try It! Choose an operation to solve each problem.

1. Dara located 2 landing spots. The first was $9\frac{1}{2}$ space-miles away. The second was $9\frac{3}{8}$ space-miles away. Which landing spot was closer?

_____

2. How much closer was the closer landing spot?

_____

3. After landing, Tanisha checked their fuel supply again. One fuel tank held $1\frac{3}{4}$ liters, another held $2\frac{2}{3}$ liters, and the third tank was empty. How much fuel did they have left?

_____

4. Even though Tanisha and Dara used less oxygen than usual, the oxygen supply was also low. The first tank held $1\frac{1}{5}$ units, and a second tank held $1\frac{7}{10}$ units. Which tank held more oxygen?

_____

5. How much oxygen did they have left?

_____

6. If they started with 40 units of oxygen, how much oxygen had they used?

_____

Name _____ Date _____

LET'S GO EXPLORING!

Strategy: Choose an Operation

Often a problem does not tell you to add or subtract to find the answer. You must read the problem carefully to choose the correct operation.

STEP 1 ▷ Read the problem.

Tanisha and Dara decided to explore the planet. On the first day they walked $3\frac{1}{2}$ space-miles. On the second day they walked $2\frac{4}{5}$ space-miles. How far did they walk in the 2 days?

STEP 2 ▷ Choose an operation.

Look for key words to help you decide which operation to use. "How far in 2 days" suggests addition. To find how far they walked, add.

STEP 3 ▷ Add. Solve the problem.

To add the fractions, you must have fractions with like denominators. Change the fractions into equivalent fractions. Reduce your answer if possible.

$3\frac{1}{2} = 3\frac{5}{10} \qquad 2\frac{4}{5} = 2\frac{8}{10}$

$3\frac{5}{10} + 2\frac{8}{10} = 5\frac{13}{10} = 6\frac{3}{10}$

They walked $6\frac{3}{10}$ space-miles on the 2 days.

Try It! Choose an operation to solve each problem.

1. On the first day Tanisha collected $3\frac{7}{8}$ pounds of rock samples. Dara collected $3\frac{3}{4}$ pounds of rock samples. Who collected more rock samples?

_____

2. How much more?

_____

3. On the third day Tanisha ate $\frac{7}{16}$ pound of food. Dara ate $\frac{3}{8}$ pound of food. How much food did they eat together?

_____

4. On the third day Tanisha and Dara walked for $2\frac{1}{2}$ hours. On the fourth day they walked for $4\frac{9}{10}$ hours. How many hours did they walk in 2 days?

_____

5. How much longer did they walk on the fourth day than on the third day?

_____

Unit 3, Improper Fractions and Mixed Numbers

Problem Solving Strategies 6, SV 0517-0

Name _____ Date _____

BACK TO EARTH!

Strategy: Use Logical Reasoning

Using logical reasoning is a way to solve a problem. It will help you decide if the answer to a problem seems reasonable.

On the fifth day Tanisha and Dara found a magic maze. It is shown on page 35. A sign by the entrance said that the maze was really a time warp. Anyone who could find all the magic numbers would magically arrive back on Earth.

Try It!

Help Tanisha and Dara get back to Earth. At each gate in the maze, match the gate letter to the problem with that letter. Then solve each problem either by reducing the fractions or changing them into equivalent fractions with higher terms. Reduce your answers if possible. If the answer matches a magic number, that gate will open. Tanisha and Dara will move closer back to Earth. If the answer does not match a magic number, Tanisha and Dara must change directions in the maze.

Here are the magic numbers:

$3\frac{7}{13}, \frac{1}{4}, 1\frac{1}{2}, \frac{9}{16}, 1\frac{1}{3}, 10\frac{7}{12}, 4\frac{3}{16}.$

Hint: You can solve all the problems to find which answers are magic numbers. Or you can use logical reasoning to choose a path for Tanisha and Dara and only try to open the gates on the path you've chosen. Good luck!

Here are the problems to solve:

A. $\frac{5}{8} - \frac{1}{8} =$ _____

B. $\frac{1}{2} - \frac{1}{12} =$ _____

C. $4\frac{9}{13} - 1\frac{2}{13} =$ _____

D. $3\frac{2}{3} + 5\frac{8}{9} =$ _____

E. $\frac{7}{16} - \frac{3}{16} =$ _____

F. $\frac{4}{5} + \frac{7}{10} =$ _____

G. $\frac{5}{16} + \frac{1}{4} =$ _____

H. $7\frac{1}{6} + 2\frac{5}{6} =$ _____

I. $\frac{15}{16} - \frac{3}{16} =$ _____

J. $2\frac{3}{4} - \frac{2}{8} =$ _____

K. $\frac{3}{5} - \frac{1}{2} =$ _____

L. $5\frac{11}{14} + 9\frac{11}{28} =$ _____

M. $\frac{1}{2} + \frac{3}{8} =$ _____

N. $\frac{8}{9} + \frac{4}{9} =$ _____

O. $\frac{4}{9} + \frac{1}{3} =$ _____

P. $\frac{9}{3} - \frac{6}{3} =$ _____

Q. $8\frac{1}{4} - 6\frac{1}{5} =$ _____

R. $1\frac{1}{2} + 9\frac{1}{12} =$ _____

S. $\frac{18}{4} - \frac{5}{16} =$ _____

T. $\frac{7}{4} + \frac{11}{6} =$ _____

    Problem Solving Strategies 6, SV 0517-0

Magic Maze

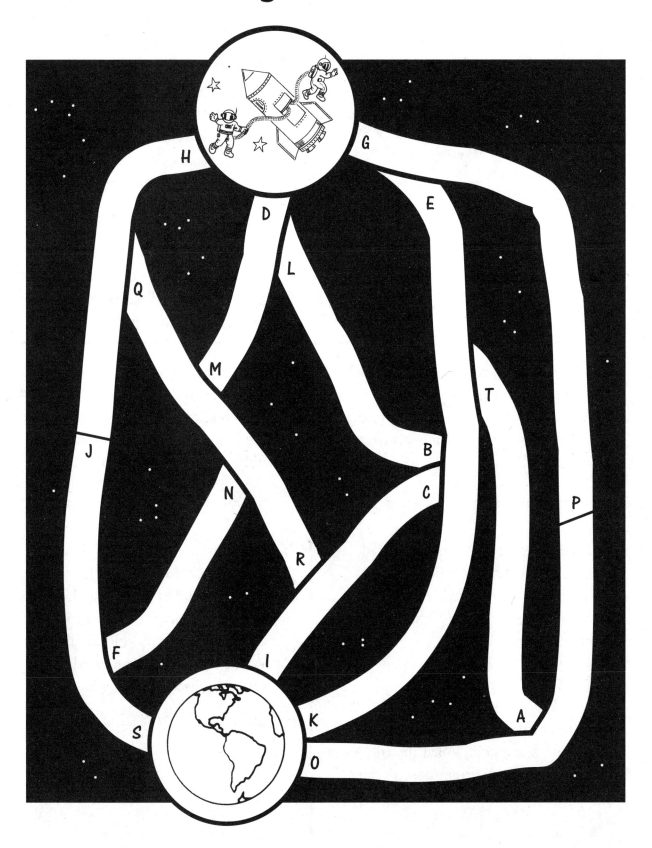

Unit 3, Improper Fractions and Mixed Numbers
Problem Solving Strategies 6, SV 0517-0

Name _____ Date _____

Unit 3 Review

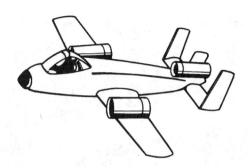

Show What You Know!

Solve each problem. Reduce your answer if possible. Identify the strategy you used.

1. Josanna made a collection of models. She used red paint on $\frac{4}{7}$ of the airplanes, $\frac{2}{3}$ of the boats, and $\frac{4}{21}$ of the cars. How many of the models were painted red?

_____

2. Omar had 5 library books. He read $1\frac{1}{8}$ of the books on Monday, $\frac{19}{16}$ on Tuesday, and $\frac{5}{4}$ on Wednesday. How much of the books did Omar read on those 3 days?

_____

3. Pedro's birthday is in 3 months. He will be 12 years old. What mixed number tells his current age in years and months?

_____

4. Mary used $3\frac{3}{8}$ feet of ribbon to decorate a package. Jeremy used $3\frac{1}{2}$ feet of ribbon to decorate a package. Who used more ribbon? How much more ribbon did that person use?

_____

5. Quinn wanted to nail two boards together. One board was $1\frac{1}{4}$ inches thick. The other board was $1\frac{1}{8}$ inches thick. Quinn has nails that measure 2 inches, $2\frac{1}{8}$ inches, and $2\frac{1}{2}$ inches. Which nail is the best length for Quinn to use? Explain your answer.

_____

Unit 3 Review, page 2

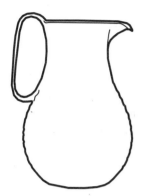

Show What You Know!

Solve each problem. Reduce your answer if possible. Identify the strategy you used.

1. Penny used 2 pitchers of juice to fill the glasses at a breakfast party. The larger pitcher filled $4\frac{3}{4}$ glasses. The smaller pitcher filled $2\frac{1}{4}$ glasses. What number sentence would you use to find out how many glasses were filled with juice?

_____

2. Mrs. Anderson needs $\frac{1}{3}$ of a fabric circle to make each flower on the quilt she is making. Are 2 circles enough to make 7 flowers?

_____

3. Tyrone worked $7\frac{2}{3}$ hours on Monday and $5\frac{1}{4}$ hours on Wednesday. How many more hours did Tyrone work on Monday than on Wednesday?

_____

4. Tyrone worked $5\frac{1}{2}$ hours on Thursday. If he had worked $1\frac{7}{8}$ hours more on Thursday, how many hours would he have worked?

_____

Extension

Use a map or a car odometer to find how far it is from your home to your school. Write that distance using a fraction or mixed number. Figure out how many miles you travel to go to and from school in 1 day, 1 week, and 1 month. Remember that you usually only go to school on weekdays and that you travel to and from school each day.

Name _____   Date _____

FLEX YOUR MATH MUSCLES

One day Flex decided to organize his house and workshop. Help Flex get organized by solving these problems.

1

Flex found some boxes of books in a closet. He had 2 boxes of adventure stories, $\frac{2}{5}$ of a box of mysteries, and $\frac{1}{5}$ of a box of comic books. How many boxes of books did he have altogether?

_____

3

Flex also found some old paint in his workshop. He had $1\frac{1}{2}$ cans of red paint, $2\frac{3}{4}$ cans of white paint, and $\frac{2}{3}$ can of black paint. How many cans of paint did he have altogether?

_____

2

Flex decided to arrange his music collection. He had 100 CDs. Of these, $\frac{1}{4}$ were country music, $\frac{2}{5}$ were rock music, and $\frac{7}{20}$ were hip-hop music. How many CDs of each kind did Flex have?

_____

4

Flex found some short pieces of board in his workshop, too. One piece was $\frac{3}{4}$ foot long, a second was $2\frac{1}{3}$ foot long, a third was $1\frac{5}{6}$ foot long, and a fourth was $3\frac{1}{2}$ feet long. Altogether, how many feet of board did Flex find?

_____

Name _____ Date _____

SPORTS FRACTIONS

Strategy: Choose an Operation

When you are working with fractions, you may not know whether to add, subtract, multiply, or divide. HINT: Sometimes a problem will ask you something like, "How much is $\frac{2}{3}$ of 3?" The word *of* is the signal to multiply.

 Read the problem.
Beto was at the driving range. He had 40 golf balls. He hit $\frac{3}{4}$ of the balls. How many balls did Beto hit?

 Identify the facts.
Beto had 40 golf balls. He hit $\frac{3}{4}$ of the balls.

STEP 3 **Choose an operation.**
Look for key words to help you decide which operation to use. The word *of* in the question means multiply.

STEP 4 **Multiply. Solve the problem.**
When you multiply fractions and whole numbers, you must first change the whole number to a fraction. $40 = \frac{40}{1}$
Then multiply the numerators. Then multiply the denominators. $\frac{3}{4} \times \frac{40}{1} = \frac{120}{4}$
Then reduce the fraction. $\frac{120}{4} = \frac{30}{1} = 30$
Beto hit 30 golf balls.

Try It!   Choose an operation to solve the following problems. Reduce the answers if possible.

1. Yolanda was shooting arrows at a target. She had 12 arrows to shoot, and $\frac{1}{3}$ of her arrows hit near the bullseye. How many arrows hit near the bullseye?

_____

2. Anthony was shooting free throws. He shot 48 times. He made $\frac{2}{3}$ of his shots. How many free throws did Anthony make?

_____

3. Maki was the pitcher for the softball team. In one game she threw 100 pitches, and $\frac{3}{5}$ of Maki's pitches were strikes. How many of Maki's pitches were strikes?

_____

4. How many of Maki's pitches were balls?

_____

Name _____ Date _____

MAIL CALL

Strategy: Choose an Operation

Sometimes solving a problem means using more than 1 operation. Decide whether to add, subtract, multiply, or divide, and then decide how to combine these operations.

 Read the problem.

Hoang sorts and delivers the hospital mail. On Monday the hospital received 165 letters. Hoang delivered $\frac{1}{3}$ of these to patients. How many letters did he deliver to patients?

 Choose an operation.

Look for key words to help you decide which operation to use. To solve the problem, you must find $\frac{1}{3}$ of 165. The word *of* signals multiply.

 Multiply. Solve the problem.

$\frac{1}{3} \times \frac{165}{1} = \frac{1 \times 165}{3 \times 1} = \frac{165}{3} = 55$

Hoang delivered 55 letters to patients.

Try It! Choose 1 or more operations to solve the problems.

1. On Monday there were 165 letters. The patients received $\frac{1}{3}$ of the mail and the doctors received $\frac{2}{5}$ of the mail. What fraction of the mail did the other departments receive?

_____

2. How many letters did the other departments receive?

_____

3. On Monday $\frac{2}{5}$ of 165 letters were for the doctors. On Tuesday $\frac{1}{4}$ of 124 letters were for the doctors. How many letters did the doctors receive on the 2 days?

_____

4. The church group donated $\frac{7}{8}$ of its 80 magazines to the hospital. Ms. Gomez used $\frac{3}{5}$ of the donated magazines for scrapbooks for the children. How many magazines were donated?

_____

5. How many magazines were used for scrapbooks?

_____

6. How many magazines were left after Ms. Gomez took some?

_____

Name _____ Date _____

AT THE HOSPITAL

Strategy: Write a Number Sentence
Number sentences help to show how numbers relate to each other.

STEP 1 ▷ **Read the problem.**
Al has a job after school at the hospital washroom. To wash the sheets Al uses $\frac{1}{4}$ cup bleach in every load. He uses $\frac{2}{3}$ as much fabric softener as bleach. How much fabric softener does he use for each load?

STEP 2 ▷ **Identify the facts.**
Al uses $\frac{1}{4}$ cup bleach in every load. He uses $\frac{2}{3}$ as much fabric softener as bleach.

STEP 3 ▷ **Write a number sentence.**
$\frac{1}{4}$ cup bleach $\times$ $\frac{2}{3}$ as much softener = total amount of softener

STEP 4 ▷ **Multiply. Solve the problem.**
Reduce the answer if possible.

$$\frac{1}{4} \times \frac{2}{3} = \frac{1 \times 2}{4 \times 3} = \frac{2}{12} = \frac{1}{6}$$

Al uses $\frac{1}{6}$ cup of fabric softener.

Try It! Write number sentences to help you solve the problems. Reduce your answers if possible.

1. Al uses $\frac{7}{8}$ cup of soap to wash the lab coats. He uses $\frac{1}{2}$ as much bleach as soap. How much bleach does he use for a load of lab coats?

_____

2. The hospital cook made soup on Saturday. She added $\frac{3}{4}$ cup of salt and $\frac{1}{3}$ as much pepper as salt. How much pepper did she use?

_____

3. For vegetable soup, the cook used $\frac{2}{5}$ as much broth as water. She used 15 cups of water. How much broth did she use?

_____

4. The hospital was staffed by 78 people on Saturday. On that day $\frac{5}{6}$ of the staff ate lunch in the cafeteria. Of these people, $\frac{3}{5}$ work in the washroom. How many of the staff who ate lunch in the cafeteria work in the washroom?

_____

Name _____ Date _____

VROOM!

Strategy: Guess and Check

One way to solve problems is to guess the answer, then check it. If it is not right, try again. Use what you learn from the first guess to make your next guess better. Guess and check until you find the right answer.

STEP 1 **Read the problem.**

Carri liked to drive miniature race cars. One day her car started with $2\frac{1}{3}$ gallons of gas. She used $\frac{1}{2}$ of the gas. How many gallons of gas did she use?

STEP 2 **Identify the facts.**

Fact 1: Carri started with $2\frac{1}{3}$ gallons of gas.

Fact 2: She used $\frac{1}{2}$ of the gas.

STEP 3 **Guess the answer.**

First you can multiply the fraction by the whole number.

$\frac{1}{2}$ of $2 = \frac{1}{2} \times \frac{2}{1} = \frac{2}{2} = 1$

Then multiply the fractions.

$\frac{1}{2} \times \frac{1}{3} = \frac{1}{6}$

Then add the two numbers. $1 + \frac{1}{6} = 1\frac{1}{6}$ gallons

STEP 4 **Check your answer.**

When multiplying a fraction by a mixed number, you can change the mixed number to a fraction.

$2\frac{1}{3} = \frac{7}{3}$

Then multiply. $\frac{7}{3} \times \frac{1}{2} = \frac{7}{6}$

Then reduce. $\frac{7}{6} = 1\frac{1}{6}$. Your answer is correct.

Try It! Guess and check to solve these problems.

1. The race track was $1\frac{3}{4}$ miles long. Carri drove $\frac{4}{5}$ of the way before her car broke down. How many miles did Carri drive?

_____

2. Once Carri was able to drive $6\frac{1}{2}$ laps before she ran out of gas. Today she only went $\frac{2}{3}$ that far before she ran out of gas. How many laps did Carri drive today before she ran out of gas?

_____

WHO WANTS PIZZA?

Strategy: Make a Model

Sometimes using a graph can help you to solve a problem more easily.

STEP 1 ▷ **Read the problem.**

Emily and Anton work at the pizza parlor. Every day they use $20\frac{1}{2}$ pounds of flour to make pizzas. They use $\frac{1}{4}$ of that flour to make pepperoni pizzas. They use $\frac{1}{8}$ of the flour to make olive pizzas. Is more flour used to make pepperoni or olive pizzas?

STEP 2 ▷ **Identify the facts.**

Fact 1: $\frac{1}{4}$ flour for pepperoni pizzas

Fact 2: $\frac{1}{8}$ flour for olive pizzas

STEP 3 ▷ **Make a model.**

$\frac{1}{4}$

$\frac{1}{8}$

STEP 4 ▷ **Use the model to compare the fractions.**

You can see that $\frac{1}{4}$ is more than $\frac{1}{8}$.

STEP 5 ▷ **Solve the problem.**

Since $\frac{1}{4}$ of the flour is more than $\frac{1}{8}$ of the flour, more flour is used for pepperoni pizzas than olive pizzas.

Try It! Make a model to help you solve these problems.

1. What fraction of the flour is used to make both the pepperoni and olive pizzas?

_____

2. What fraction of the flour is used to make other kinds of pizzas?

_____

3. Is more flour used to make pepperoni and olive pizzas or other kinds of pizzas?

_____

4. How many pounds of flour are used to make pepperoni pizzas?

_____

Name _____ Date _____

MAKING TACOS

Strategy: Write a Number Sentence

Writing a number sentence can help you to solve problems more easily.

 Read the problem.

Luis was making tacos. He put $1\frac{1}{3}$ teaspoons of pepper in the taco meat. He added $1\frac{1}{2}$ times as much salt as pepper. How many teaspoons of salt did he use?

STEP 2 Identify the facts.

Fact 1: Luis used $1\frac{1}{3}$ teaspoons of pepper.

Fact 2: He used $1\frac{1}{2}$ times as much salt as pepper.

STEP 3 Write a number sentence to solve the problem.

$1\frac{1}{3}$ teaspoons pepper $\times$ $1\frac{1}{2}$ times more salt = total teaspoons of salt

When multiplying a mixed number by a mixed number, change both mixed numbers into improper fractions.

$1\frac{1}{3} = \frac{4}{3}$ $\qquad$ $1\frac{1}{2} = \frac{3}{2}$

Multiply the numerators, and then the denominators.

$\frac{4}{3} \times \frac{3}{2} = \frac{12}{6}$

Reduce the answer.

$\frac{12}{6} = 2$

Luis used 2 teaspoons of salt.

Try It! Write number sentences to help you solve these problems.

1. Luis also made beans to eat. He used $1\frac{7}{8}$ cups of beans. Then he added $3\frac{1}{3}$ times as much water as beans. How many cups of water did he use?

   _____

2. Luis made a rice dish, too. For spices, he used $1\frac{3}{4}$ teaspoons of cumin. Then he added $1\frac{1}{3}$ times as much garlic salt as cumin. How many teaspoons of garlic salt did he use?

   _____

Name _____ Date _____

GLUB, GLUB!

Strategy: Identify Substeps
Sometimes a problem requires several steps to solve.

STEP 1 **Read the problem.**
Ben could hold his breath underwater for $1\frac{1}{4}$ minutes. Ashley could hold her breath $1\frac{1}{3}$ times longer than Ben. How many seconds could Ashley hold her breath?

STEP 2 **Identify the facts.**
Fact 1: Ben could hold his breath for $1\frac{1}{4}$ minutes.

Fact 2: Ashley could hold her breath $1\frac{1}{3}$ times longer than Ben.

STEP 3 **Identify the substeps.**
Substep 1: First you must figure how many minutes Ashley could hold her breath. Multiply the two mixed numbers.

Substep 2: Then you must figure how many seconds Ashley could hold her breath. Multiply the number of minutes by 60 seconds.

STEP 4 **Work the substeps. Solve the problem.**
First figure the minutes.

$1\frac{1}{4} \times 1\frac{1}{3} = \frac{5}{4} \times \frac{4}{3} = \frac{20}{12} = 1\frac{8}{12} = 1\frac{3}{4}$

Ashley could hold her breath for $1\frac{3}{4}$ minutes. Now figure the seconds.

$1\frac{3}{4}$ minutes $\times$ 60 seconds per minute $= \frac{7}{4} \times \frac{60}{1} = \frac{420}{4} = 105$

Ashley could hold her breath for 105 seconds.

Try It! Identify the substeps to solve each problem.

1. Cheryl could swim a lap in $1\frac{3}{5}$ minutes. Sid took $1\frac{1}{4}$ times longer than Cheryl. How many seconds faster could Cheryl swim a lap than Sid?

_____

2. April swam a lap in $2\frac{1}{3}$ minutes using the crawl stroke. When she used the dog paddle, she took $1\frac{1}{2}$ times longer. How many seconds did it take April to swim a lap using the dog paddle?

_____

3. How many minutes faster could she swim the crawl than the dog paddle?

_____

Name _____ Date _____

Unit 4 Review

Show What You Know!

Solve each problem. Reduce your answer if possible. Identify the strategy you used.

1. Regina bowled a score of 154 points. She calculated that $\frac{1}{7}$ of her points were from spares and strikes. How many of her points were from spares and strikes?

_____

2. Jimar bought 2 oranges at the market. The first orange weighed $\frac{2}{3}$ pound. The second orange weighed $\frac{3}{4}$ pound. How much more did the second orange weigh?

_____

3. Nathan traded 15 sports cards. Out of those cards $\frac{1}{5}$ of them were baseball cards. How many baseball cards did Nathan trade?

_____

4. Charlene did her homework in $2\frac{1}{4}$ hours. She spent $\frac{1}{3}$ of that time doing science homework. How much time did she spend doing her science homework?

_____

5. During a timed math test, Daniel completed $3\frac{1}{2}$ multistep problems. On the same test, Francine completed $\frac{1}{4}$ more problems than Daniel. How many problems did Francine complete?

_____

Unit 4 Review, page 2

Strategy: Make a Model

Ingredients in Granola

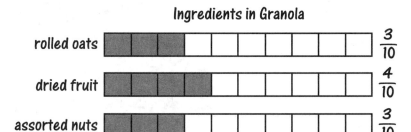

rolled oats $\frac{3}{10}$

dried fruit $\frac{4}{10}$

assorted nuts $\frac{3}{10}$

Show What You Know!

Make a model to solve the problems. Reduce your answer if possible.

1. Ben made $6\frac{1}{2}$ cups of granola. What fraction of the granola is made from dried fruit and assorted nuts?

_____

2. What fraction of the granola is made from other ingredients?

_____

3. How many cups of dried fruit does Ben need to make the granola?

_____

4. If Ben cuts the recipe to make $\frac{1}{2}$ as much, how much granola would he make?

_____

5. If Ben cuts the recipe to make $\frac{1}{2}$ as much, will that change the fraction of the recipe that is rolled oats, dried fruit, and assorted nuts? Explain your answer.

_____

Extension . . . .

Use a cookbook to look up a simple recipe. Determine how much of each ingredient you would need if you cut the recipe to make $\frac{1}{2}$ as much.

Name _____ Date _____

FLEX YOUR MATH MUSCLES

To exercise your brain, work problems that are short and quick.

1

1. How much is $\frac{2}{3}$ of $\frac{3}{4}$? _____

2. How much is $\frac{2}{3}$ of $\frac{3}{4}$ of 8 ? _____

3. How much is $\frac{2}{3}$ of $\frac{3}{4}$ of 50 ? _____

2

Do you see the pattern? Finding a pattern can help you to solve problems more easily.

4. How much is $\frac{1}{2}$ of 96 ? _____

5. How much is $\frac{1}{2}$ of 48 ? _____

6. How much is $\frac{1}{2}$ of 24 ? _____

7. How much is $\frac{1}{2}$ of 12 ? _____

3

See, another pattern. Now try this one.

8. $90 \times$ _____ $= 60$

9. $60 \times$ _____ $= 40$

4

OK, now see if you can discover what the pattern is here.

10. How much is $2 \times 1{,}234 \times \frac{1}{2}$? _____

11. How much is $4 \times 1{,}234 \times \frac{1}{4}$? _____

12. How much is $3 \times 1{,}234 \times \frac{1}{3}$? _____

Unit 4, Multiplying Fractions
Problem Solving Strategies 6, SV 0517-0

Name _____ Date _____

SIGN IN, PLEASE!

Strategy: Write a Number Sentence

Number sentences show how numbers relate to each other. Writing a number sentence can help you to solve a problem more easily.

STEP 1 ▷ **Read the problem.**

Lina signed in 8 salespeople at the front desk this week. To find the number of people who might visit in a month, she must divide the number of people who visit in a week by $\frac{1}{4}$. This fraction equals 1 week or $\frac{1}{4}$ of a month. How many salespeople might Lina sign in this month?

STEP 2 ▷ **Identify the facts.**

Fact 1: She signed in 8 people.

Fact 2: 1 week = $\frac{1}{4}$ of a month

STEP 3 ▷ **Write a number sentence.**

8 salespeople $\div \frac{1}{4}$ = salespeople who might sign in this month

STEP 4 ▷ **Divide. Solve the problem.**

First change the whole number into an improper fraction. $8 = \frac{8}{1}$

To divide by a fraction, invert the second fraction (divisor) to find its reciprocal. The reciprocal of $\frac{1}{4}$ is $\frac{4}{1}$. Then multiply the first fraction by the reciprocal of the second fraction. Reduce your answer if possible.

$8 \div \frac{1}{4} = \frac{8}{1} \div \frac{4}{1} = \frac{32}{1} = 32$

32 salespeople might sign in this month.

Try It! Write a number sentence to solve each problem.

1. Lina wants to know how many salespeople might sign in this year. She must divide the number of salespeople who sign in this month by $\frac{1}{12}$. This fraction represents 1 month, or $\frac{1}{12}$ of a year. This month 32 salespeople signed in. How many salespeople can Lina expect in a year?

_____

2. Lina puts each visitor's name on a badge. Each badge uses $\frac{1}{6}$ of a sheet of tagboard. She has 4 sheets of tagboard. How many badges can she make?

_____

3. A quarter is 25 cents, or $\frac{1}{4}$ of a dollar. How many quarters are in $5.00?

_____

Problem Solving Strategies 6, SV 0517-0

Name _____ Date _____

THINGS TO SHARE

Strategy: Work Backward

Sometimes you need to work backward to solve a problem. Write a number sentence to help you.

STEP 1 ▷ Read the problem.

Every week Miriam buys a bouquet of flowers and shares them with 2 other people in her office. This week she divided $\frac{3}{5}$ of the bouquet among all 3 of them, but she kept the rest of the bouquet (all the yellow flowers) for herself. What fraction of the bouquet did Miriam keep for herself?

STEP 2 ▷ Identify the facts.

Fact 1: There are 3 people in the office.

Fact 2: Miriam divided $\frac{3}{5}$ of the bouquet among the 3 of them.

Fact 3: Miriam kept the rest of the bouquet, the yellow flowers, for herself.

STEP 3 ▷ Write a number sentence.

$\frac{3}{5} \div 3 +$ yellow flowers $=$ part of bouquet Miriam kept

STEP 4 ▷ Work backward to solve the problem.

a. Change the whole number into an improper fraction. $3 = \frac{3}{1}$

b. Invert the second fraction (divisor) to find its reciprocal. The reciprocal of $\frac{3}{1}$ is $\frac{1}{3}$.

c. To divide by a fraction, multiply the first fraction by the reciprocal of the second fraction. Reduce the answer if possible.

$\frac{3}{5} \div 3 = \frac{3}{5} \div \frac{3}{1} = \frac{3}{5} \times \frac{1}{3} = \frac{3}{15} = \frac{1}{5}$

Each person shared $\frac{1}{5}$ of the bouquet.

d. To find the fraction of the bouquet that were yellow flowers, subtract the fraction from the whole.

$1 - \frac{3}{5} = \frac{5}{5} - \frac{3}{5} = \frac{2}{5}$

The yellow flowers were $\frac{2}{5}$ of the bouquet.

e. To find the fraction of the bouquet that Miriam kept, add her part of the shared fraction of the bouquet to the yellow flowers.

$\frac{1}{5}$ (Miriam's share) $+ \frac{2}{5}$ (yellow flowers) $= \frac{3}{5}$

Miriam kept $\frac{3}{5}$ of the whole bouquet for herself.

Problem Solving Strategies 6, SV 0517-0

Name _____ Date _____

THINGS TO SHARE, part 2

Strategy: Work Backward

Try It! Write a number sentence for each problem to show how the numbers are related to each other. Then work backward to solve each problem. Reduce your answers if possible.

1. Miriam, Claudia, and Francisco work in the hospital's medical records office. On Friday afternoon they still had to finish checking $\frac{2}{3}$ of the patient files. They divided the files evenly so they could finish the work. What fraction of the remaining files did each person check?

_____

2. On Tuesday Claudia brought in $\frac{3}{4}$ of a dozen doughnuts. She shared them equally with Miriam and Francisco. What fraction of the dozen doughnuts did each person get?

_____

3. How many doughnuts did each person get?

_____

4. On Wednesday Miriam brought in $\frac{1}{2}$ of a pizza. She shared it with Claudia. What fraction of the pizza did each person get?

_____

5. On Thursday Francisco brought in $\frac{1}{2}$ of a gallon of juice. Miriam, Claudia, and he each drank an equal amount of the juice. What fraction of the juice did each person drink?

_____

6. On Friday Miriam's friend Bob brought in $\frac{5}{6}$ of a box of candy. He shared it equally with Miriam, Claudia, and Francisco. What fraction of the candy did each person get?

_____

7. If the whole box of candy had 24 pieces, how many pieces of candy did each person get?

_____

8. Later Francisco brought in 1 dozen cookies. He shared the cookies equally with Miriam and Claudia. What fraction of the cookies did each person get?

_____

Name _____ Date _____

CHEERFUL VOLUNTEERS

Strategy: Make a Model
Sometimes a model helps to organize the information in a problem. Be sure to include all the important facts.

STEP 1 ▷ Read the problem.
Three students visited the hospital's elderly patients. They divided their time evenly so each would have a turn. Altogether, they worked for a total of $5\frac{2}{5}$ hours. How much time did each student spend with elderly patients?

STEP 2 ▷ Identify the facts.
There were 3 students. They divided their time evenly.
They worked a total of $5\frac{2}{5}$ hours.

STEP 3 ▷ Make a model.
Each box is divided into fifths.
Each box represents 1 hour.

$$\boxed{|||||} + \boxed{|||||} + \boxed{|||||} + \boxed{|||||} + \boxed{|||||} + \boxed{|||||} = \frac{27}{5}$$

STEP 4 ▷ Divide. Solve the problem.
Altogether, there are 27 fifths, or $\frac{27}{5}$.
Divide the boxes into 3 equal groups. Circle each group.
There are 3 groups. So each group contains $\frac{9}{5}$. $\quad \frac{9}{5} = 1\frac{4}{5}$
Each student worked $1\frac{4}{5}$ hours.

Try It! Make a model to help you solve each problem.

1. For a snack, the 3 students ate $3\frac{3}{4}$ ounces of carrots. If they shared the carrots equally, how many ounces of carrots did each student eat?

_____

2. The 3 students pooled their money and bought $7\frac{1}{3}$ dozen flowers from the gift shop. If they divided the flowers equally among 4 patients, how many dozen flowers did each patient get?

_____

3. How many flowers did each patient get?

_____

4. If the students used $4\frac{4}{5}$ sheets of paper to write notes about 6 patients, how many sheets did they use for each patient?

_____

Name _____ Date _____

A MULTICULTURAL FEAST

Strategy: Identify Extra Information

Some problems have too much or too little information. If there is too much information, cross out the information that doesn't help you solve the problem. Then work the problem.

 Read the problem.

Sharona worked in the hospital. She asked everyone to bring something for the multicultural party. She brought $6\frac{2}{3}$ packages of rice cakes and $4\frac{7}{8}$ pounds of tofu. If she divided the packages of rice cakes by $\frac{1}{3}$ to make more packages, how many smaller packages of rice cakes would she have?

STEP 2 **Identify the facts you need and circle them. Identify the facts you don't need and cross them out.**

Need: Sharona brought $6\frac{2}{3}$ packages of rice cakes.

Need: She divided the packages of rice cakes by $\frac{1}{3}$.

Don't need: She brought $4\frac{7}{8}$ pounds of tofu.

 Decide which operation to use. Solve the problem.

Divide to find the number of smaller packages of rice cakes. Change the mixed number into an improper fraction: $6\frac{2}{3} = \frac{20}{3}$. Invert the second fraction (divisor) to find the reciprocal: $\frac{1}{3}$ becomes $\frac{3}{1}$. To divide, multiply the improper fraction by the reciprocal. Reduce the answer. $\frac{20}{3} \times \frac{3}{1} = \frac{60}{3} = 20$

She would have 20 smaller packages of rice cakes.

Try It! Identify key information. Cross out the extra facts. Then solve the problems.

1. Mr. Olson brought Swedish meatballs to the party. He bought 2 pounds of beef. His recipe makes $9\frac{1}{2}$ large meatballs. If he divides the number of meatballs by $\frac{1}{4}$, he will have enough smaller meatballs for everyone. How many smaller meatballs can he make?

_____

2. Simone made Greek baklava for the party. She used $\frac{1}{2}$ cup of nuts and $\frac{3}{4}$ cup of honey in the recipe. She cut 10 pieces from 1 pan. If she divided the pieces by $\frac{1}{3}$, how many slices would she have?

_____

Name _____ Date _____

EVERYDAY HOSPITAL TASKS

Strategy: Choose an Operation

Some problems do not tell you to add, subtract, multiply, or divide. Read the problem carefully to help you to choose the correct operation.

 Read the problem.

Pat has $15\frac{2}{5}$ yards of gauze to make bandages. Each bandage uses $1\frac{2}{5}$ yards. How many bandages can Pat make?

 Identify the facts.

Pat has $15\frac{2}{5}$ yards of gauze. Each bandage uses $1\frac{2}{5}$ yards of gauze.

 Choose an operation.

Divide $15\frac{2}{5}$ by $1\frac{2}{5}$ to find the number of bandages Pat can make.

STEP 4 **Divide. Solve the problem.**

$15\frac{2}{5} \div 1\frac{2}{5} = \frac{77}{5} \div \frac{7}{5} = \frac{77}{5} \times \frac{5}{7} = \frac{385}{35} = 11$

Pat can make 11 bandages.

Try It! Choose an operation to solve each problem.

1. Pat has $56\frac{1}{4}$ pounds of plaster. If 1 cast uses $3\frac{3}{4}$ pounds of plaster, how many casts can Pat make?

_____

2. Pat can wrap a bandage with $1\frac{1}{10}$ yards of tape. If he has $8\frac{4}{5}$ yards of tape, how many bandages can he wrap?

_____

3. The nursery uses $2\frac{1}{4}$ packages of cotton balls every day. There are $13\frac{1}{2}$ packages on the shelf. How many days' supply of cotton balls does the nursery have?

_____

4. The emergency room uses $9\frac{3}{4}$ times more cotton balls in a month than the nursery uses in a day. If the nursery uses $2\frac{2}{3}$ packages in a day, how many packages does the emergency room use in a month?

_____

Name _____ Date _____

FUN WITH PATTERNS!

Strategy: Look for a Pattern

Some problems can be solved by recognizing a pattern. Look for a pattern. Use the pattern to help you solve the problem more easily.

STEP 1 **Read the problem.**

What are the missing numbers in this pattern?

dividend		divisor						quotient		reduced quotient
$\frac{3}{4}$	$\div$	$\frac{1}{2}$	$=$	$\frac{3}{4}$	$\times$	$\frac{2}{1}$	$=$	$\frac{6}{4}$	$=$	$1\frac{1}{2}$
$\frac{3}{4}$	$\div$	$\frac{1}{4}$	$=$	$\frac{3}{4}$	$\times$	$\frac{4}{1}$	$=$	$\frac{12}{4}$	$=$	3
$\frac{3}{4}$	$\div$	$\frac{1}{8}$	$=$	$\frac{3}{4}$	$\times$	$\frac{8}{1}$	$=$	$\frac{24}{4}$	$=$	6
$\frac{3}{4}$	$\div$	___	$=$	$\frac{3}{4}$	$\times$	___	$=$	___	$=$	___

STEP 2 **Find the pattern.**

Determine the relationship of the numbers. Each divisor is $\frac{1}{2}$ smaller than the previous divisor. Each quotient is twice as much as the previous quotient.

STEP 3 **Write the rule for the pattern.**

Divide each divisor by $\frac{1}{2}$.

STEP 4 **Use the rule. Solve the problem.**

Fill in the missing numbers in the table.

$\frac{3}{4} \div \frac{1}{16} = \frac{3}{4} \times \frac{16}{1} = \frac{48}{4} = 12$

Try It! Find a pattern. Use the pattern to help you solve the problem.

1. The nurses held a contest. The children had to roll a ball down the hall. To award points, they divided the length of the roll by $\frac{1}{5}$. How many points did each child score? Fill in the blanks in the table.

child	dividend		divisor						quotient		points scored
Ruben	$\frac{5}{6}$	$\div$	$\frac{1}{5}$	$=$	$\frac{5}{6}$	$\times$	$\frac{5}{1}$	$=$	$\frac{25}{6}$	$=$	$4\frac{1}{6}$
Milly	$\frac{4}{6}$	$\div$	$\frac{1}{5}$	$=$	$\frac{4}{6}$	$\times$	$\frac{5}{1}$	$=$	___	$=$	___
Chan	$\frac{}{6}$	$\div$	$\frac{1}{5}$	$=$	$\frac{}{6}$	$\times$	$\frac{5}{1}$	$=$	___	$=$	___
Rosa	$\frac{2}{6}$	$\div$	$\frac{1}{5}$	$=$	$\frac{2}{6}$	$\times$	$\frac{5}{1}$	$=$	___	$=$	___
Skip	$\frac{}{6}$	$\div$	$\frac{1}{5}$	$=$	$\frac{}{6}$	$\times$	$\frac{5}{1}$	$=$	___	$=$	___

Name _____ Date _____

Unit 5 Review

Show What You Know!

Solve each problem. Reduce your answer if possible. Identify the strategy you used.

1. Felipe had $\frac{1}{2}$ pound of dog food. If he divided it equally between his 2 dogs, how much food did each dog get?

_____

2. Dana, Susan, Greg, and Frank worked on a mural for 2 hours. They only had time to paint $6\frac{1}{2}$ feet of the mural. If each person painted an equal amount of the mural, how much did each person paint?

_____

3. Constance placed pepperoni on $\frac{3}{4}$ of the pizza she made. If she and 2 friends shared the pepperoni pizza, how much did each person eat?

_____

4. Min equally divided $\frac{4}{5}$ of a cake among 4 people. How much cake did each person get?

_____

5. If Min divided the remaining piece of cake between 2 people, how much cake did each of these people get?

_____

6. Andrés had $\frac{7}{8}$ can of popcorn. He divided it equally with Octavio and Carlos. How much popcorn did each boy get?

_____

Name _____ Date _____

Unit 5 Review, page 2

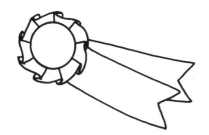

Strategies
- Work Backward
- Look for a Pattern

Show What You Know!

Function Table

RULE: Divide by $\frac{1}{8}$

IN	OUT	Reduced
$\frac{1}{12}$	$\frac{8}{12}$	$\frac{2}{3}$
$\frac{2}{12}$	$\frac{16}{12}$	$1\frac{1}{3}$
$\frac{3}{12}$	$\frac{24}{12}$	2
$\frac{4}{12}$	$\frac{32}{12}$	$2\frac{2}{3}$
$\frac{5}{12}$		
$\frac{6}{12}$		
$\frac{7}{12}$		
$\frac{8}{12}$		

Solve each problem. Reduce your answer if possible. Identify the strategy you used.

1. Paul made a function table to show a pattern when dividing by $\frac{1}{8}$. If Paul puts in $\frac{5}{12}$, what will come out of the function table? What is the reduced answer?

   _____

2. If Paul puts in $\frac{6}{12}$, what will come out of the function table? What is the reduced answer?

   _____

3. If Paul puts in $\frac{7}{12}$, what will come out of the function table? What is the reduced answer?

   _____

4. If Paul puts in $\frac{8}{12}$, what will come out of the function table? What is the reduced answer?

   _____

Extension

Find out how many days you go to school each year. Put that number over 365 days to determine what fraction of the year you are in school. Divide that fraction by $\frac{1}{4}$.

Unit 5, Dividing Fractions
Problem Solving Strategies 6, SV 0517-0

Name _____ Date _____

FLEX YOUR MATH MUSCLES

One evening Flex was sitting by his backyard pond. He was thinking about all the math he had learned recently. Help Flex review by solving these problems.

1

In his job as a delivery driver, Flex had worked a total of 97.5 hours. He had earned $5.70 an hour. How much were his total earnings from his delivery job?

_____

3

Flex's tomatoes also did well. He harvested $10\frac{1}{2}$ pounds of tomatoes. He gave $\frac{1}{3}$ of these to his neighbors. How many pounds of tomatoes did he give to his neighbors?

_____

2

Flex's garden had done well. He had harvested $7\frac{1}{4}$ pounds of squash and $8\frac{2}{3}$ pounds of beans. How many total pounds of these vegetables did he harvest?

_____

4

Flex admired the flowers in his garden. He had 12 yellow flowers and 9 red flowers. What was the ratio of red flowers to yellow flowers?

_____

Problem Solving Strategies 6, SV 0517-0

Name _____ Date _____

10 IS A POWERFUL NUMBER

Strategy: Use a Pattern

To multiply decimals by 10, 100, or 1,000, move the decimal point to the right as many places as there are zeros. Sometimes you have to write zeros in the answer to move the decimal point the correct number of places.

0.63×10: move the decimal point 1 place to the right = 6.3
0.95×100: move the decimal point 2 places to the right = 95.0
$0.335 \times 1,000$: move the decimal point 3 places to the right = 335.0
0.7×100: move the decimal point 2 places to the right and write a zero in the product = 70.0

 Read the problem.
Harry bought 10 bags of peanuts at the game. Each bag cost $0.25. What was Harry's total cost for the peanuts?

 Identify the facts.
Each bag of peanuts cost $0.25. Harry bought 10 bags.

 Multiply. Solve the problem.
Multiply the decimal by the whole number. Use the pattern to move the decimal point. $0.25 \times 10 = \$2.5 = \$2.50$ (Add a zero to make the money amount correct.) Harry paid $2.50 for the peanuts.

Try It! Use the pattern of multiplying decimals by moving the decimal point. Add zeros if necessary.

1. Jesse paid $12.00 for a ticket to the game. If 1,000 people bought tickets at that price, how much money was collected?

_____

2. Each program cost $2.00. Only 100 people bought a program. How much money was collected for the programs?

_____

3. Mr. Young bought his scout troop baseball pennants. Each pennant cost $5.00. How much did he spend for 10 pennants?

_____

4. The teams played an average of 3.5 hours per game. How many hours would they play in 10 games?

_____

Problem Solving Strategies 6, SV 0517-0

Name _____ Date _____

EVERYTHING IN ITS PLACE!

Strategy: Look for a Pattern

When you multiply decimals by whole numbers or decimals by decimals, multiply as if both numbers are whole numbers. To place the decimal point in the product, use this pattern: Count the total number of decimal places in the multiplier and multiplicand. You will then have that many decimal places in the product. Sometimes you need to add zeros in the product to place the decimal point correctly.

STEP 1 ▷ **Read the problem.**
Dad bought a membership to a fitness club for 3.5 months. Each month cost $55.70. How much did Dad pay for the membership?

STEP 2 ▷ **Identify the facts.**
The membership cost $55.70 per month for 3.5 months.

STEP 3 ▷ **Multiply. Solve the problem.**
Multiply the numbers. Count the decimal places in both numbers. Place the decimal point. When working with money, you should have only 2 numbers to the right of the decimal point.
$55.70 a month × 3.5 months = $194.950 = $194.95
Dad paid $194.95 for the membership.

 Try It! Count the number of decimal places to put the decimal point in the correct place. Add zeros if necessary.

1. The club restaurant charges $1.52 for a glass of juice. Each carton holds 4.5 glasses. How much money will the restaurant make with 1 carton of juice?

_____

2. Members can swim in the pool for 10.5 hours each day. The pool is open 6 days a week. How many hours can members swim in the pool each week?

_____

3. Each of the 1,000 club members receives an average of 2.5 announcements each month. How many announcements does the club mail each month?

_____

4. At the club, babysitting costs $5.50 for 1 hour. How much would babysitting cost for 3.5 hours?

_____

Name _____ Date _____

LET'S BAKE SOME CUPCAKES!

Strategy: Write a Number Sentence

A number sentence shows how numbers relate to each other. Writing a number sentence can help you to solve the problem more easily. Be sure to count the number of decimal places in the multiplier and multiplicand to place the decimal point correctly.

STEP 1 **Read the problem.**
A recipe calls for 1.25 cups of flour for 1 dozen cupcakes. If you are baking 2.5 dozen cupcakes, how many cups of flour will you need?

STEP 2 **Identify the facts.**
1.25 cups of flour make 1 dozen cupcakes.

STEP 3 **Write a number sentence.**
1.25 cups for 1 dozen × 2.5 dozen = total cups of flour

STEP 4 **Multiply. Solve the problem.**
Multiply the decimals. Count the decimal places to put the decimal point in the correct location.
1.25 × 2.5 = 3.125 You will need 3.125 cups of flour for 2.5 dozen cupcakes.

Try It!

Write a number sentence to help you solve each problem. Round your answers to the nearest 0.5.

1. The recipe calls for 6.33 ounces of milk for 1 dozen cupcakes. How many ounces of milk would you need for 4.5 dozen cupcakes?

_____

2. The recipe also calls for 3.6 ounces of berries for 1 dozen cupcakes. How many ounces of berries would you need for 2.25 dozen cupcakes?

_____

3. You decide to put 0.25 ounces of sparkles on each dozen cupcakes. How many ounces of sparkles would you need for 10.5 dozen cupcakes?

_____

4. Grandma wants to bake 0.5 dozen cupcakes. She needs one-half the amount of ingredients as for 1 dozen cupcakes. How much flour, milk, and berries will she need to bake 0.5 dozen cupcakes? (Hint: Multiply each amount for 1 dozen cupcakes by 0.5.)

_____

Problem Solving Strategies 6, SV 0517-0

WHAT'S IN STORE?

Strategy: Identify Substeps

Some problems use more than one operation. List the facts and plan the operations you will use to solve the problem.

STEP 1 ▸ Read the problem.

Mike and Kim worked at the grocery store after school. Mike worked 2.5 hours a day. Kim worked 1.5 times longer than Mike each day. If Kim earned $5.20 an hour, how much would she earn for a day's work?

STEP 2 ▸ Identify the substeps.

Substep 1: First you must find how many hours Kim worked a day. Multiply.

Substep 2: Then you must figure how much Kim earned for a day's work. Multiply again.

STEP 3 ▸ Work the substeps. Solve the problem.

2.5 hours Mike worked × 1.5 times longer = 3.75 hours Kim worked each day

3.75 hours Kim worked × $5.20 an hour = $19.50 a day Kim earned for her day's work

Try It! Identify the substeps to help you solve each problem.

1. Mike stocked shelves at the store. He could put 0.75 of a box of cans on a shelf 1.5 feet long. If he had a shelf 10.5 feet long, how many boxes of cans could he put on it?

   _____

2. How many boxes of cans could he put on a shelf 7.5 feet long?

   _____

3. Kim liked to work in the flower shop at the store. She would wrap each bunch of flowers with 0.6 feet of ribbon. If she had to wrap 12 bunches of flowers, how many feet of ribbon would she use?

   _____

4. If the ribbon cost $0.30 a foot, how much would it cost for Kim to wrap the 12 bunches of flowers?

   _____

Name _____ Date _____

LET'S GO TO THE ZOO!

Strategy: Look for a Pattern

There is a pattern you can use when you divide a decimal by a multiple of 10. To divide a decimal by 10, 100, or 1,000, move the decimal point in the dividend to the left as many places as there are zeros in the divisor.

$0.75 \div 10$: move the decimal point 1 place to the left = 0.075
$25.9 \div 100$: move the decimal point 2 places to the left = 0.259
$658.4 \div 1,000$: move the decimal point 3 places to the left = 0.6584

STEP 1 ▷ Read the problem.
You have 3.5 pounds of peanuts to feed 10 monkeys at the zoo. If you give each monkey an equal amount, how much will each monkey get?

STEP 2 ▷ Identify the facts.
3.5 pounds of peanuts for 10 monkeys. How much for each monkey? *Each* signals division.

STEP 3 ▷ Divide. Solve the problem.
Divide the decimal by the whole number. Use the pattern to move the decimal point.
3.5 pounds ÷ 10 monkeys = 0.35 pounds
Each monkey gets 0.35 pounds of peanuts.

Try It! To solve each problem, use the pattern to move the decimal point.

1. The zoo buys 1.25 tons of hay each week to feed 10 elephants. Each elephant eats the same amount of hay. How much hay does each elephant eat in a week?

_____

2. The zoo has 100 snakes. The snakes eat 15.5 pounds of food each day. If each snake eats the same amount, how much does each snake eat in a day?

_____

3. The zoo has 1,000 birds in the bird house. The birds eat 675.75 pounds of seed in a week. If each bird eats the same amount, how much seed would 1 bird eat in a week?

_____

4. The refreshment stand at the zoo sells lemonade. In 100 days, 5,386.5 gallons of lemonade were sold. How many gallons of lemonade were sold each day?

_____

Problem Solving Strategies 6, SV 0517-0

Name _____ Date _____

WATERMELON, ANYONE?

Strategy: Identify Substeps

To divide a decimal by a whole number or a decimal, place the decimal point in the quotient above the decimal point in the dividend. Then divide as you do with whole numbers. Sometimes you need to add zeros in the quotient to line up the decimal points.

 Read the problem.

The farmer brought watermelons to the market. He sold 15 melons for $54.75. It cost him $1.12 to grow and harvest each melon. How much profit did he make on the sale of 1 melon?

 Identify the substeps.

Substep 1: To figure how much it cost him to grow and harvest the melons, multiply $1.12 × 15.

Substep 2: Subtract this amount from the amount he made at the market. The difference will be his profit for the sale of 15 melons.

Substep 3: Then you must divide his total profit by 15 melons to get his profit on 1 melon.

 Work the substeps. Solve the problem.

$1.12 × 15 = $16.80 (his cost to grow and harvest 15 melons)

$54.75 − $16.80 = $37.95 (his profit on the sale of 15 melons)

$$\begin{array}{r} \$2.53 \\ 15\overline{)\$37.95} \end{array}$$ The farmer made $2.53 profit on each melon.

Try It! Identify the substeps to solve these problems. When you divide, line up the decimal point in the quotient with the decimal point in the dividend. (You can use a calculator to check your answers.)

1. You have 2 watermelons. One melon weighs 6.93 pounds, and the other weighs 5.61 pounds. If you cut both melons into slices weighing 0.33 pound each, how many slices can you serve altogether?

_____

2. Watermelons are on sale. You can buy 3 melons for $6.99 at 1 store. Each melon weighs 12 pounds. At another store, watermelons are $0.15 per pound. These melons weigh 12 pounds each, too. Which watermelons are the better buy?

_____

Name _____ Date _____

PARTY TIME!

Strategy: Choose an Operation

Some problems do not tell you to add, subtract, multiply, or divide, or how to combine these operations. You must read the problem carefully to choose the operation. In these problems you will have to decide whether to multiply or divide.

STEP 1 ▷ **Read the problem.**
Twelve children ate birthday cake. Each piece of cake weighed 0.22 pounds. One half the cake is left. How much did the whole cake weigh?

STEP 2 ▷ **Choose an operation.**
Identify key words to help you decide which operation to use. *Whole* signals addition. It is easier to multiply 12×0.22 than to add 0.22 twelve times. To find how much the whole cake weighed, multiply.

STEP 3 ▷ **Multiply. Solve the problem.**
12 pieces $\times$ 0.22 pounds per piece = 2.64 pounds = $\frac{1}{2}$ of the cake
2.64 pounds $\times$ 2 halves = 5.28 pounds
The whole cake weighed 5.28 pounds.

Try It! Choose an operation to solve each problem.

1. Guests at the party drank chocolate milk. Each pitcher held 38 ounces. If 12 guests each drank 9.5 ounces of milk, how many pitchers of milk did they drink?

_____

2. One snack at the party was a bag of corn chips that weighed 16.5 ounces. If 15 guests each ate an equal amount, how many ounces of chips did each guest eat?

_____

3. Party favors cost $1.45 for each guest. If there were 17 guests at the party, how much did the party favors cost altogether?

_____

4. Friends ate the remaining 2.64 pounds of cake. It was cut into equal pieces that weighed 0.33 pound each. How many friends ate the remaining cake?

_____

Name _____ Date _____

Unit 6 Review

Show What You Know!

Solve each problem. Identify the strategy you used.

1. Raul bought 10 tickets at the movie theater. Each ticket cost $3.50. How much did Raul pay for all the tickets?

_____

2. If Raul bought 100 movie tickets over the course of a year, how much would he pay?

_____

3. Every day Lela jogged 3.6 miles. How many miles did she jog in 14 days?

_____

4. Jean sold 100 candy bars for a school fundraiser. Each candy bar cost $1.50. How much money did Jean raise for her school?

_____

5. Donny was preparing for a party and bought a block of cheese that weighed 18.75 pounds. He cut wedges of cheese. Each wedge weighed 0.15 pounds. How many wedges of cheese did Donny cut?

_____

6. Brenda and Brandon belonged to a book club. Each month the twins shared a new book that they bought for $1.95. How much money will they spend in 12 months?

_____

7. One morning the temperature was 6.5°F. By noon, the temperature was 12.5°F. What was the change in temperature?

_____

Unit 6 Review, page 2

Show What You Know!

Solve each problem. Identify the strategy you used.

1. Mr. Samuelson works in a small chocolate shop. He fills the first 12 boxes with 2.35 pounds of chocolate in each box. He fills the next 12 boxes with 1.55 pounds of chocolate in each box. How many pounds of chocolate does Mr. Samuelson use to fill the 24 boxes?

_____

2. Toni used a special saw to cut a slice from a small round stone. She measured the diameter of the slice and found out it was 0.56 inches. She looked at it under a microscope and magnified the stone 10 times. How large does the diameter appear to be when it is magnified 10 times?

_____

3. On Monday, Javier earned $157.50 cutting 7 lawns that were about the same size. On Tuesday, he earned $56.25 cutting 3 lawns that were smaller than the ones he cut on Monday. How much did he charge for each lawn on Monday and Tuesday?

_____

4. Caleb earned $2.50 per hour for babysitting his cousins. He babysat for 2.5 hours on Friday, 4.5 hours on Saturday, and 4.0 hours on Sunday. How much money did Caleb earn babysitting his cousins for those 3 days?

_____

5. A miner found 3 gold nuggets, each weighing 1.24 ounces. What is the total combined weight of the gold nuggets?

_____

Extension

Measure the perimeter of the top of your desk to the nearest 0.25 inch. What would be the perimeter of the top of your desk if you could enlarge it by 2.5 times?

Name _____ Date _____

FLEX YOUR MATH MUSCLES

Flex Mathews has had lots of different jobs. Help him solve these problems about his job as a delivery driver.

1

For a while Flex worked as a delivery driver. Every day he had to drive from the warehouse to the store and back. The round trip was 7.75 miles. If he drove the round trip 10 times a day, how many miles would he drive in a day?

_____

2

How many miles would he drive in 5 days?

_____

3

On one trip Flex had to deliver 100 boxes that weighed 0.75 pounds each. What was the total weight of his delivery?

_____

4

On another trip Flex had to deliver 1,000 bottles that each held 0.3 ounces of perfume. How many ounces of perfume did he deliver?

_____

5

On 1 delivery Flex carried a box that weighed 31.5 pounds. He knew the box held 14 hammers. How much did each hammer weigh?

_____

6

Flex earned $5.70 an hour as a delivery driver. If he worked 17.5 hours one week, how much money did he earn?

_____

Name _____ Date _____

RATIOS ARE LIKE FRACTIONS

Strategy: Model a Ratio

A ratio is a way of comparing numbers or quantities. To figure the ratio, compare the parts to the whole. The ratio is found by dividing one number by another. The ratio is the quotient of the two numbers or quantities. Ratios can be written in several ways. For example, the ratio of 1 thing compared to 2 things can be written as 1 to 2, 1:2, or $\frac{1}{2}$.

 Read the problem.
What is the ratio of triangles to all shapes in this illustration?

STEP 2 Identify the facts.
The number of triangles is 3. The total number of shapes is 9.

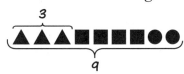

STEP 3 Model the ratio. Solve the problem.
To find the ratio, divide the number of triangles by the total number of shapes. Reduce your answer if possible.

$3 \div 9 = \frac{3}{9} = \frac{1}{3}$ The ratio is 3 to 9, or 1 to 3. It can also be written as 1:3 or $\frac{1}{3}$.

Try It! Model the ratios to find the ratios in each problem. Write the ratios in 3 ways. Reduce your answers if possible.

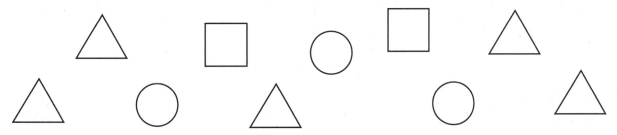

1. What is the ratio of triangles to total shapes?

_____

2. What is the ratio of squares to total shapes?

_____

3. What is the ratio of circles to squares?

_____

4. What is the ratio of circles to triangles?

_____

Name _____ Date _____

ARE THESE THE SAME?

Strategy: Set Up a Proportion

Sometimes you will have two ratios that have the same value. These are called equal ratios, or proportions. Use cross-products to decide if two ratios are equal, or proportional. You can conclude that if the cross-products are equal, the ratios are equal.

 Read the problem.
There are 9 coaches for 45 players on the soccer team. Last year there were 5 coaches for 25 players. Are the ratios proportional?

 Set up a proportion.
First find the ratio of coaches to players. Reduce your answer if possible.

9 coaches to 45 players = $\frac{9}{45} = \frac{1}{5}$

5 coaches to 25 players = $\frac{5}{25} = \frac{1}{5}$

$\frac{1}{5} = \frac{1}{5}$

The ratios are proportional.

Try It! Set up proportions to solve the problems. Write *yes* if the ratios are equal or *no* if they are not equal.

1. Bananas are on sale at 5 for $1.00. Is the ratio of 5 bananas for $1.00 equal to the ratio of 15 bananas for $3.00?

   _____

2. Grapes are on sale at $0.69 per pound. Is this equal to 3 pounds of grapes for $2.75?

   _____

3. Oranges are on sale at 2 pounds for $0.90. Is this equal to 3 pounds of oranges for $1.35?

   _____

4. Apples are on sale for $0.75 per pound. Is this equal to 4 pounds of apples for $2.90?

   _____

Name _____ Date _____

LOOK HERE!

Strategy: Make a Table
Making a table will help you to figure equal ratios more easily.

STEP 1 **Read the problem.**
Ned went to the mall to rent some videos. He had $6.00. He knew that videos rented for $2 each. How many videos can Ned rent?

videos	1	2	3
cost	$2	$4	?

STEP 2 **Identify the facts.**
Ned had $6.00. One video cost $2.00.

STEP 3 **Make a table. Solve the problem.**
Making a table can help you solve the problem. A ratio table shows equal ratios. If 1 video costs $2, then 2 videos cost $4. How much do 3 videos cost?

$\frac{1}{\$2} = \frac{2}{\$4}$ and $\frac{1}{\$2} = \frac{3}{\$6}$

By multiplying cross-products, you can see that 3 videos would cost $6. Since Ned had $6.00, he could rent 3 videos.

Try It! Make a ratio table to help you solve each of these problems.

1. Ned also went to the video arcade. It costs Ned $1.00 to play 2 games. How much would it cost Ned to play 10 games?

_____

2. How much would it cost Ned to play 7 games?

_____

3. How much would it cost Ned to play 5 games?

_____

4. Ned ended up at the music store. CDs were on sale at 2 CDs for $22.00. How much would 6 CDs cost?

_____

5. How much would 8 CDs cost?

_____

6. How much would 1 CD cost?

_____

Problem Solving Strategies 6, SV 0517-0

Name _____ Date _____

THIS IS TO THAT

Strategy: Set Up a Proportion

An equal ratio is also called a proportion. Proportions are used to solve problems with equal ratios. Use cross-products to find proportions.

 Read the problem.
Jake can buy 8 apples for $2. How much will 4 apples cost?

 Set up a proportion.
To find how much 4 apples will cost, you set up a proportion and cross-multiply to find an equal ratio.

STEP 3 **Multiply. Solve the problem.**
To find an equal ratio, find the cross-products:

$$\frac{8 \text{ apples}}{\$2} = \frac{4 \text{ apples}}{\$?} \qquad 8 \times \$? = 4 \times \$2 \qquad 8 \times \$? = \$8 \qquad \$? = \$1$$

Jake can buy 4 apples for $1.

Try It! Use proportions and cross-products to help you solve each problem.

1. Jake can buy 5 oranges for $1. How much would 20 oranges cost?

_____

2. A dozen pencils costs $0.96. How much does 1 pencil cost?

_____

3. How much do 6 pencils cost?

_____

4. Mr. Barnes uses 1 quart of paint to make 4 signs for the store. How many quarts of paint would he need to make 10 signs?

_____

5. Jake can jog the 2 miles to the store in 30 minutes. How long would it take Jake to jog 3 miles?

_____

6. A store is selling 3 bars of soap for $4. How much will 9 bars of soap cost?

_____

7. Henry has $10 to spend on comic books. The store sells 2 comic books for $4. How many comic books can Henry buy?

_____

HOW HIGH IS THAT?

Strategy: Set Up a Proportion

Proportions can be used to find the heights of objects that are too tall to measure easily. Use a proportion to help you solve the problem.

 Read the problem.
A 5-meter post casts a 3-meter shadow. A flag pole casts a 15-meter shadow. How tall is the flag pole?

 Set up a proportion.
Use t to equal the height of the flag pole. Then set up a proportion.

$$\frac{5 \text{ m post}}{3 \text{ m shadow}} = \frac{t \text{ (flag pole)}}{15 \text{ m shadow}}$$

STEP 3 **Cross-multiply. Solve the problem.**
Use cross-products to find the value of t.

$$5 \times 15 = 3 \times t \qquad 75 = 3t \qquad \frac{75}{3} = t \qquad 25 = t$$

The flag pole is 25 meters tall.

Try It! Use a formula and proportions to help you solve these problems.

1. Stu is 6 feet tall. He is standing by a tree. His shadow is 4 feet long. The tree's shadow is 12 feet long. How tall is the tree?

_____

2. The school building casts a shadow 15 feet long. A traffic sign is 6 feet tall and casts a shadow 3 feet long. What is the height of the school building?

_____

3. A street light is 7 meters tall. It casts a shadow 2 meters long. A water tower near the street light casts a shadow 8 meters long. How tall is the water tower?

_____

4. Antoine thought the basketball hoop was too high. It was supposed to be 10 feet high. Antoine was 5 feet tall and his shadow was 3 feet long. The shadow of the hoop was 7 feet long. Was the hoop too high?

_____

Name _____ Date _____

1 IN 100

Strategy: Define Percent

The ratio of any number to 100 is called a percent. Percent is written as %.

Percents can also be written as a decimal. Change a percent to a decimal by moving the decimal point 2 places to the left. Drop the % sign.

Change a decimal to a percent by moving the decimal point 2 places to the right. Add the % sign.

Fractions can also be changed to percents. Find an equivalent fraction with 100 as the denominator. Then write the number as a percent.

30 out of 100 = $\frac{30}{100}$ = 30% = 0.30

1 out of 100 = $\frac{1}{100}$ = 1% = 0.01

100 out of 100 = $\frac{100}{100}$ = 100% = 1

7 out of 20 = $\frac{7}{20}$ = $\frac{35}{100}$ = 35% = 0.35

Try It! Solve these problems. Write the percentages.

1. Seven out of every 10 students wore jackets on the field trip. What percent of students wore jackets?

_____

2. What percent of students did not wear jackets?

_____

3. Eight of the 50 people on the bus were parents. What percent of the people were parents?

_____

4. What percent were not parents?

_____

5. Three out of 4 students took sandwiches in their sack lunches. What percent of the students took sandwiches?

_____

6. What percent did not take sandwiches?

_____

Name _____ Date _____

SOME OF YOUR BUSINESS

Strategy: Identify Substeps

Percents are used often in business. Stores often have items on sale. The sale price is some percentage off the regular price. The difference in price is called a discount. Governments often charge a sales tax on certain items. The sales tax is added to the price of the item. So knowing percentages can make you a better shopper!

STEP 1 ▷ **Read the problem.**

Jacy found a bike that was on sale for 25% off the regular price of $80. There was a 6% sales tax on the selling price. What was the total cost of the bike?

STEP 2 ▷ **Make a plan.**

First find the sale price of the bike. Multiply the regular price by 25% (0.25) and subtract the product from the regular price. Then find the sales tax. Multiply the sale price by 6% (0.06). Then add the sale price and the sales tax to get the total cost.

STEP 3 ▷ **Solve the problem.**

$80.00 × 0.25 = $20.00

$80.00 (regular price) − $20.00 (discount) = $60.00 (sale price)

$60.00 × 0.06 (sales tax) = $3.60 (tax)

$60.00 + $3.60 = $63.60   The total cost was $63.60.

Try It!   Solve these problems about percentages.

1. Jacy also bought a bike helmet that was on sale for 20% off the regular price of $39.00. The sales tax was 6%. What was the total cost of the helmet?

_____

2. The store was having a sale on bike shorts. Jacy found a pair that was 15% off the regular price of $12.00. The sales tax was 6%. What was the total cost of the shorts?

_____

3. Jacy rode her new bike to the library. On the way she stopped to buy a soda for $0.59. The sales tax was 6%. What was the total cost of the soda?

_____

4. The library had 3,000 books. Of these, 35% were fiction. How many books were nonfiction?

_____

5. How many books were fiction?

_____

Name _____ Date _____

Unit 7 Review

Show What You Know!

Solve each problem. Identify the strategy you used.

1. Petula sells 10 newspapers for $5.00 and 20 newspapers for $10.00. How much money does she collect if she sells 30 newspapers? How much money does she collect if she sells 40 newspapers?

_____

2. Arthur took a math test that had 20 problems. He got 16 correct. Maggie took a different math test. She got 8 correct out of 10 problems. Is the ratio of 16 correct answers out of 20 problems equal to the ratio of 8 correct answers out of 10 problems? Explain your answer.

_____

3. Victor made 3 greeting cards in 1 hour. How many cards could he make in 3 hours? Write a number sentence to help you solve the problem.

_____

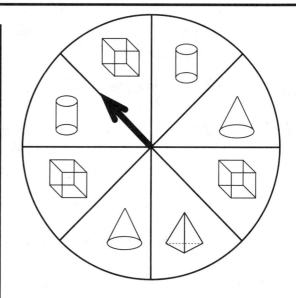

4. What is the ratio of cubes to total shapes?

_____

5. What is the ratio of pyramids to cones?

_____

Name _____ Date _____

Unit 7 Review, page 2

Strategies
- Model a Ratio
- Set Up a Proportion
- Make a Table
- Define Percent
- Identify Substeps

Show What You Know!

Solve each problem. Identify the strategy you used.

1. Carolyn collects stamps. She can put 8 stamps on each page of her album. What formula would you use to find out how many stamps she can put on 12 pages of her album?

_____

2. A store had 100 apples on display. There were 35 green apples, 40 red apples, and 25 yellow apples. What percent of apples were green?

_____

3. What percent of the 100 apples in the store display were red?

_____

4. What percent of the 100 apples in the store display were yellow?

_____

5. For every 5 toys that Girard made, Celia made 3. What formula would you use to show how many toys Girard made if Celia made 27?

_____

6. Keith measured the plant he grew for the Science Fair. Before adding any special vitamins, it measured 2.35 inches. The first week he added one set of vitamins. The plant grew by 6%. The second week he added a different set of vitamins, and the plant grew by 2%. What did the plant measure after the first and second weeks? Round your answer to the nearest hundredth.

_____

Extension

Survey 20 students to find out how many like football, soccer, baseball, volleyball, or basketball best. Write ratios to compare the data and percentages to describe the data.

Name _____ Date _____

FLEX YOUR MATH MUSCLES

When Flex is not busy on a project, he likes to work in his garden.

1

Flex has 75 vegetable plants in his garden. Of these, 24% are bean plants. How many bean plants does Flex have?

_____

4

Flex has 8 tomato plants. Of these, 6 are cherry tomato plants. What percentage of Flex's tomato plants are cherry tomato plants?

_____

2

Flex has 8 tomato plants and 5 squash plants. What is the ratio of tomato plants to squash plants? Write the ratio 3 ways.

_____

5

What percentage of Flex's 75 vegetable plants are cherry tomato plants?

_____

3

What is the ratio of squash plants to tomato plants? Write the ratio 3 ways.

_____

6

The 8 tomato plants were on sale for $0.30 each. There was also a 7% sales tax. What was the total cost of the 8 tomato plants?

_____

Name _____ Date _____

CHANCES ARE

Strategy: Use a Drawing

Probability is the chance or likelihood that something will happen. To find probability, you must first determine the total number of possible outcomes, or chances of happening. Then you must compare the likelihood of 1 event happening in relation to the total outcomes. This comparison is stated as a ratio.

Suppose you are playing a game that uses a spinner. There are 6 numbers on the spinner. You can spin a 1, 2, 3, 4, 5, or 6. That means there are 6 possible outcomes. When you spin, though, you will land on only 1 number. That means there is only 1 happening, or event. Your chance, or probability, of spinning any given number, such as a 2, is 1 chance in 6, or $\frac{1}{6}$.

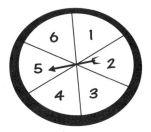

$$\frac{1}{6} = \frac{\text{event}}{\text{total number of possible outcomes}}$$

The chance of the spinner landing on 1 of 2 numbers, such as a 2 or a 3, is the sum of the separate probabilities. The probability of rolling a 2 is $\frac{1}{6}$. The probability of rolling a 3 is also $\frac{1}{6}$. But the probability of rolling a 2 or a 3 is 2 chances in 6, $\frac{2}{6}$ or $\frac{1}{3}$. (Reduce your answer if possible.)

Try It! Use the drawing of the spinner above to solve these problems.

1. What is the probability the spinner will land on a 6?

_____

2. What is the probability the spinner will land on an odd number?

_____

3. What is the probability the spinner will land on a 1, 2, or 3?

_____

4. What is the probability the spinner will land on a number greater than 1?

_____

Problem Solving Strategies 6, SV 0517-0

TRY YOUR LUCK

Strategy: Use a Drawing

| A 1 | B 2 | C 3 | A 4 | B 5 | C 1 | A 2 | B 3 | C 4 | A 5 |

Suppose you are playing a game that uses 10 cards. Each card has a number and a letter on it. Because there are 10 cards, there are 10 possible outcomes. What is the probability you will pick a card with an A or 1?

The chance of picking an A or 1 is the sum of the separate possibilities.

probability of picking an A = $\frac{4}{10}$ or $\frac{2}{5}$

probability of picking a 1 = $\frac{2}{10}$ or $\frac{1}{5}$

probability of picking A or 1 = $\frac{2}{5} + \frac{1}{5} = \frac{3}{5}$

Try It!

Use the drawings of the cards above to solve the following problems. Reduce your answers if possible.

1. What is the probability you will pick a card with a B?

_____

2. What is the probability you will pick a card with a 5?

_____

3. What is the probability you will pick a card with an odd number?

_____

4. What is the probability you will pick a card with a B or a 3?

_____

Name _____ Date _____

WHAT COLOR IS YOUR BACKPACK?

Strategy: Use a Table

Probability is sometimes called relative frequency. A table makes it easier to show the ratio of the probable events to the total number of outcomes.

Alicia did a survey. She asked her classmates what color backpack they had. She put the results in a frequency table.

There are 30 students in Alicia's class, so there are 30 possible outcomes.

Frequency Table	
Color	Number of students
blue	8
red	5
black	4
green	7
gray	6

Try It! Use the table above to solve these problems. Reduce your answers if possible.

1. What color of backpack is the most popular?

_____

2. What color of backpack is the least popular?

_____

3. What is the probability that Karen has a red backpack?

_____

4. What is the probability that Armando has a gray backpack?

_____

5. What is the probability that Shenille has a green or a black backpack?

_____

6. What is the probability that Larry does not have a blue backpack?

_____

7. What is the probability that Sondra has a black or gray backpack?

_____

8. What is the probability that Raul does not have a green backpack?

_____

Name _____ Date _____

WHAT'S YOUR FREQUENCY?

Strategy: Make a Table

To find the relative frequency, or probability, of an event, write the ratio of the frequency of the event to the total number of possible outcomes.

For a school survey, Josh asked 50 of his classmates how many pets they owned. He put the results in a frequency table.

What is the probability a student owns 4 pets?

probability of 4 pets $= \frac{1}{50} = \frac{\text{frequency of event}}{\text{total possible outcomes}}$

Pets Owned	
Event	Frequency
0 pets	5
1 pet	18
2 pets	20
3 pets	6
4 pets	1
Total	**50**

Try It!   Use the table to find the probability. Reduce your answers if possible.

1. What is the probability a student owns 2 pets?

_____

2. What is the probability a student owns 3 pets?

_____

3. What is the probability a student owns 2 or 3 pets?

_____

4. What is the probability Bill has no pets?

_____

5. What is the probability Karen owns fewer than 4 pets?

_____

6. What is the probability Alvin owns more than 1 pet?

_____

7. What is the probability a student doesn't have a pet?

_____

8. What is the probability a student has more than 2 pets?

_____

Unit 8, Probability
Problem Solving Strategies 6, SV 0517-0

Name _____ Date _____

WHAT'S YOUR PREDICTION?

Strategy: Set Up a Proportion

You can use relative frequencies, or probabilities, to make predictions.

Josh added a column of relative frequencies to his table. Now he can use the relative frequencies to make predictions.

To predict how many out of 100 students own 3 pets, he wrote a formula, called a proportion, and solved it.

$\frac{n}{100} = \frac{6}{50}$

$n \times 50 = 6 \times 100 \qquad n \times 50 = 600 \qquad n = 12$

Pets Owned		
Event	Frequency	Relative Frequency
0 pets	5	$\frac{1}{10}$
1 pet	18	$\frac{9}{25}$
2 pets	20	$\frac{2}{5}$
3 pets	6	$\frac{3}{25}$
4 pets	1	$\frac{1}{50}$
Total	**50**	**1**

Try It! Use the table and proportions to make predictions.

1. How many out of 100 students own 2 pets?

_____

2. How many out of 100 students own 2 or 3 pets?

_____

3. How many out of 200 students own 1 pet?

_____

4. How many out of 100 students own fewer than 4 pets?

_____

5. How many out of 500 students own 1 pet?

_____

6. How many out of 200 students own 3 or 4 pets?

_____

Problem Solving Strategies 6, SV 0517-0

Name _____ Date _____

BATTER UP!

Strategy: Write a Number Sentence

The study of statistics deals with collecting, organizing, and analyzing mathematical facts, or data. You see statistics everywhere you turn, especially in elections and sports. Using a number sentence can help you to figure statistics more easily.

One important term in statistics is *average*. Sports statistics use a player's average in many categories. An average is usually figured by dividing the number of successful attempts by the total number of attempts.

For example, a baseball batting average is the number of safe hits (successful attempts) divided by the number of times at bat (total number of attempts). A 0.300 batting average is the same as 30% and means the hitter gets 30 hits in 100 times at bat, or 300 hits in 1,000 times at bat.

30 hits ÷ 100 at-bats = 0.300 batting average
300 hits ÷ 1,000 at-bats = 0.300 batting average

Try It!   Write a number sentence to help you find the averages for these problems.

1. Sal had 45 hits in 180 at-bats. What is his batting average?

_____

2. Sara had 50 hits in 150 at-bats. What is her batting average?

_____

3. In 12 baseketball games, Shana made 22 free throws in 33 tries. What is her free-throw shooting average?

_____

4. The school soccer team has played 12 games and won 7. What is the team's winning average?

_____

5. Mary Kate is the pitcher on the softball team. In 5 games, she pitched to 175 batters and struck out 75 of them. What is Mary Kate's strike-out average?

_____

Problem Solving Strategies 6, SV 0517-0

WHAT DO YOU THINK?

Strategy: Use a Table

You have probably heard about surveys and polls. Surveys and polls ask a selected number of people, called a sample, some questions. Because a poll cannot really ask 10 million people what they think, the poll will ask 1,000 people and then project the results to the larger group.

Food	Girls	Boys
Pizza	7	8
Hamburger	5	4
Taco	5	6
Hot Dog	3	2

The sample can be random, meaning there is no real order to the choosing of the people. Or the sample can be scientific, meaning the poll asks representative people.

For example, you want to conduct a lunchroom poll about favorite foods. You could use a random sample, where you ask every third or fourth student what he or she likes to eat. Or you could use a scientific sample, where you ask an even number of boys and girls.

You decide to ask 20 girls and 20 boys in the sixth grade what their favorite food is. You put the results in a table.

Try It! Use the table and proportions to project, or predict, results for larger groups.

1. If 7 out of 20 girls like pizza, how many girls out of 100 would probably like pizza?

_____

2. If 6 out of 20 boys like tacos, how many boys out of 200 would probably like tacos?

_____

3. If 5 out of 40 boys and girls like hot dogs, how many boys and girls out of 120 would probably like hot dogs?

_____

4. If 20 out of 40 boys and girls like hamburgers and tacos, how many boys and girls out of 400 would probably like hamburgers and tacos?

_____

Name _____ Date _____

Unit 8 Review

Strategies
- Use a Drawing
- Use a Table
- Set Up a Proportion
- Write a Number Sentence

Show What You Know!

Solve each problem. Identify the strategy you used.

1. Kendall has 3 pennies, 2 nickels, 5 dimes, and 1 quarter in her change purse. If she pulls out a coin without looking, what is the probability that she will pick a nickel?

_____

2. Suki noticed that 3 out of 10 students have blonde hair. What formula would she use to find how many out of 100 students have blonde hair?

_____

3. Zelda entered 10 art contests. She got first-place ribbons in 4 of them. What is her average for winning first-place at art contests?

_____

Ice Cream Flavor	Boys	Girls
Chocolate	12	10
Vanilla	5	4
Strawberry	3	6

4. Winnie took a survey of 20 sixth-grade boys and 20 sixth-grade girls to see whether they liked chocolate, vanilla, or strawberry ice cream best. If 12 out of 20 boys like chocolate ice cream, how many boys out of 100 would probably like chocolate ice cream?

_____

5. If 4 out of 20 girls like vanilla ice cream, how many girls out of 100 would probably like vanilla ice cream?

_____

Name _____   Date _____

Unit 8 Review, page 2

Strategy: Use a Drawing

Key
R = Red
B = Blue
Y = Yellow
G = Green

Show What You Know!

Use the drawing to solve the problems.

1. Quincy put 10 colored tiles in a brown paper bag. He asked Aunt Julia to pull out a tile from the bag without looking. What is the probability that Aunt Julia's tile will be orange?

_____

2. What is the probability that the first tile Aunt Julia picks will be green?

_____

3. What is the probability that the first tile Aunt Julia picks will be red or blue?

_____

4. What is the probability that the first tile Aunt Julia picks will be yellow or green?

_____

5. Quincy removes all of the red tiles from the bag. Now what is the probability that Aunt Julia will pick a yellow tile?

_____

6. With the red tiles removed, what is the probability that the first tile Aunt Julia picks will be blue?

_____

Extension ....

Count all of your shirts. How many are mostly blue? mostly green? mostly red? If you pick a shirt without looking, what is the probability that, when you get dressed tomorrow, you will pick a shirt that is mostly blue? mostly green? mostly red?

Name _____ Date _____

Flex likes problems about probabilities and statistics. Help him solve these problems.

1

Flex's friend Barry did not study for his true/false test. What is the probability he will get the first question right?

_____

2

There are 10 questions on the true/false test. What is the probability Barry will get any 1 question right?

_____

3

Flex is rolling a die in a board game. The die is a cube with 6 faces, each with a number from 1 to 6. Flex needs to roll a 5. What is the probability that Flex will roll a 5?

_____

What is the probability that Flex will not roll a 5?

_____

4

Flex likes baseball. He knows that Cy Young was the winningest pitcher in the history of professional baseball. He won 511 games and lost 313. What was his winning average?

_____

5

Cy Young played for 21 years, from 1890 to 1911. What was the average number of games he won each year during that period? Round your answer to the nearest whole number.

_____

6

Flex played softball in the city league. He was a good batter. One season he got 96 hits in 246 times at bat. What was Flex's batting average?

_____

What was Flex's average for not getting hits?

_____

Unit 8, Probability
Problem Solving Strategies 6, SV 0517-0

Name _____ Date _____

WHAT SHAPE ARE YOU IN?

Strategy: Use a Drawing

Geometry is the mathematics of shapes. Triangles are 3-sided shapes with 3 angles. The sum of the 3 angles is 180 degrees.

Hint: The symbol for degrees is °.

Try It! Read the description of each kind of triangle. Then label the drawing with the correct type of triangle.

Equilateral triangles have 3 equal sides and 3 equal angles. Isosceles triangles have 2 equal sides and 2 equal angles. Scalene triangles have 3 unequal sides and 3 unequal angles. Right triangles have 1 angle of 90°. Obtuse triangles have 1 angle greater than 90°.

1.

1a. _____ 1b. _____ 1c. _____

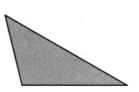

1d. _____ 1e. _____

Try It! Complete the description of each type of triangle. Either circle the correct answer or fill in the blank.

2. In an equilateral triangle, each angle is _____°.

3. In a right triangle, the sum of the 2 smaller angles is _____°.

4. In an obtuse triangle, the sum of the 2 smaller angles is (greater, less) than 90°.

5. Draw a triangle. Label what kind of triangle it is.

Problem Solving Strategies 6, SV 0517-0

Name _____ Date _____

WHAT'S IN THE CORNER?

Strategy: Use a Drawing

Quadrilaterals are 4-sided figures. The sum of the 4 angles in a quadrilateral is 360°.

Try It! Read the description of each kind of quadrilateral. Then label the drawing with the correct type.

Rectangles have 4 right angles of 90° each. In a rectangle, opposite sides are equal and parallel. Squares are rectangles with 4 equal and parallel sides. Parallelograms have opposite sides that are equal and parallel. Rectangles and squares are parallelograms, but not all parallelograms are rectangles or squares. Trapezoids have no 90° angles. In a trapezoid 1 pair of opposite sides is equal and not parallel. The other pair of opposite sides is unequal and parallel.

1.

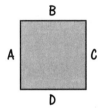   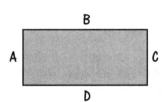

1a. _____   1b. _____

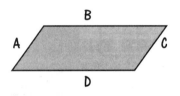   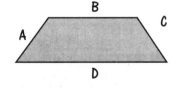

1c. _____   1d. _____

Try It! Use the drawings above to complete the description of each type of quadrilateral. Circle the correct answer or fill in the blank.

2. In the rectangle, 2 parallel sides are (A, C or C, D).

3. In a square, the sum of 2 opposite angles is _____.

4. In the parallelogram, 2 sides that are equal and parallel are (A, C or B, C).

5. In the trapezoid, the sides that are unequal and parallel are (B, D or A, C).

6. Draw a quadrilateral and label what type it is.

Problem Solving Strategies 6, SV 0517-0

Name _____ Date _____

AREA CODE

Strategy: Use a Formula

You can find the perimeter and area of any geometrical shape using a formula. The perimeter is the sum of the length of the sides. The area is the total space. The area is expressed in square units, such as square inches.

A = Area   P = Perimeter   W = Width   H = Height
S = Side   B = Base (the bottom of a triangle)

Rectangle: To find the perimeter, use the formula P = 2W + 2H.
     To find the area, use the formula A = W × H.

Square: To find the perimeter, use the formula P = S × 4.
     To find the area, use the formula A = S × S or A = W × H.

Triangle: To find the perimeter, use the formula P = S + S + S.
     To find the area, use the formula $A = \frac{1}{2}B \times H$.

 STEP 1 **Read the problem.**
Find the area of this rectangle.

STEP 2 **Choose a formula.**
To find the area of a rectangle, use the formula A = W × H.

STEP 3 **Replace the letters with numbers and multiply. Solve the problem.**
A = W × H   A = 4 feet × 5 feet   A = 20 square feet

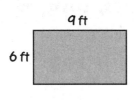

figure 1

figure 2

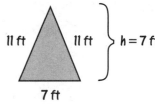

figure 3

Try It! Use the formulas and drawings above to find the area and perimeter of each shape.

1. Figure 1: Area = _____ Perimeter = _____
2. Figure 2: Area = _____ Perimeter = _____
3. Figure 3: Area = _____ Perimeter = _____
4. Draw a rectangle, square, or triangle. Label it with dimensions. Then find the area and perimeter of your shape.

Unit 9, Geometry
Problem Solving Strategies 6, SV 0517-0

Name _____ Date _____

ROUND AND ROUND WE GO!

Strategy: Use a Formula

You can find the circumference and area of a circle by using a formula. To find the circumference of a circle, use the formula C = πd. In the formula, *d* is the diameter of the circle. The diameter is a line between two points on the circumference, or the outer edge of a circle. The diameter passes through the center of the circle. The π in the formula is equal to 3.14.

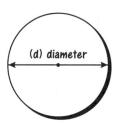

To find the area of a circle, use the formula A = πr^2. The radius, or *r*, is the distance from the center of the circle to the circumference. The radius is equal to $\frac{1}{2}$ of the diameter.

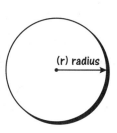

HINT—The little 2 by the *r* means to square the number, or multiply it by itself.

 Read the problem.
Find the circumference and area of a circle with a diameter of 8 inches.

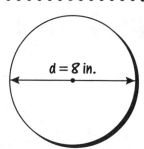

 Identify the facts.
The circle's diameter is 8 inches.

STEP 3 **Use a formula.**
To find the circumference of a circle, the formula is C = πd.
To find the area of a circle, the formula is A = πr^2.

STEP 4 **Replace the letters with numbers, and multiply. Solve the problem.**
To find the circumference:
π = 3.14   d = 8   C = 3.14 × 8 = 25.12
The circumference is 25.12 inches.

To find the area:
π = 3.14   r = $\frac{1}{2}$ × d = $\frac{1}{2}$ × 8 = 4   r^2 = 4 × 4 = 16
A = 3.14 × 16 = 50.24
The area is 50.24 square inches.

Problem Solving Strategies 6, SV 0517-0

ROUND AND ROUND WE GO, part 2

Strategy: Use a Formula

Try It! Use a formula and make a drawing to help you solve these problems.

1. The diameter of a circle is 18 inches. What is the radius?

   _____

2. A wheel has a diameter of 14 inches. What is the circumference of the wheel?

   _____

3. An apple pie has a radius of 5 inches. What is the area of the pie?

   _____

4. If you cut the pie into 8 pieces, what part of the circumference (in inches) will each piece be?

   _____

5. A circle has a radius of 6 inches. What is the circumference?

   _____

6. A circle has a diameter of 16 inches. What is the area of the circle?

   _____

7. A small pizza has a diameter of 8 inches. A large pizza has a diameter of 14 inches. What is the difference in area between the large pizza and the small pizza?

   _____

8. A tabletop has a circumference of 188.4 inches. What is the radius of this round tabletop?

   _____

9. A garden pond has a circumference of 6 feet. Another pond has a circumference of 8 feet. Which pond has the larger area?

   _____

93

PROBLEMS WITH THE THIRD DIMENSION!

Strategy: Identify Substeps

A three-dimensional figure has width, depth, and height. An example is a box. On a rectangular box, there are 6 surface areas, or faces. The top and bottom are the same size in area, the front and back are the same size, and the remaining 2 sides are the same size. To find the total surface area of the box, you must find the area of the top, the front, and a side. Add these areas, then multiply by 2 to find the area of all 6 faces.

 Read the problem.
Find the total surface area of a rectangular box with these dimensions in inches:
W = 4; H = 2; L = 3.

 Identify the substeps.
Substep 1: First you must find the area of the top, the front, and a side.
Substep 2: Then add the 3 areas.
Substep 3: Then multiply by 2.

 Work the substeps. Solve the problem.
Find the areas.
Top A = 4 × 3 = 12 square inches
Front A = 4 × 2 = 8 square inches
Side A = 3 × 2 = 6 square inches
Add the areas.   12 + 8 + 6 = 26 square inches
Then multiply by 2.   26 × 2 = 52 square inches
The rectangular box has a total surface area of 52 square inches.

Try It!   Identify the substeps, then solve these problems.

1. A rectangular box is 8 inches wide, 10 inches long, and 4 inches high. What is the total surface area of the box?

_____

2. A square box (also called a cube) has a height of 5 inches. What is the total surface area of the cube?

_____

Name _____ Date _____

HOW MUCH IS IN THERE?

Strategy: Use a Formula

Volume is the amount of space inside a three-dimensional object. Volume is measured in cubic units, for example, cubic inches.

To find the volume of a rectangular box, use the formula
$V = W \times L \times H$.

STEP 1 **Read the problem.**
What is the volume of a rectangular box with these dimensions in inches: W = 4; L = 3; H = 2?

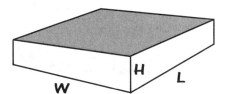

STEP 2 **Use a formula.**
To find the volume of a rectangular box, the formula is $V = W \times L \times H$.

STEP 3 **Replace the letters with numbers and multiply. Solve the problem.**
$V = 4 \times 3 \times 2 = 24$ The volume of the box is 24 cubic inches.

Try It! Use a formula to solve these problems.

1. A square box (cube) has a width of 4 inches. What is the volume of the cube?

_____

2. A rectangular box has a height of 6 inches, a width of 10 inches, and a length of 7 inches. What is the volume of the box?

_____

3. A cube has a height of 7 inches. What is the volume of the cube?

_____

4. A small shed has a width of 10 feet, a length of 12 feet, and a height of 8 feet. What is the volume of the shed?

_____

Name _____ Date _____

Unit 9 Review

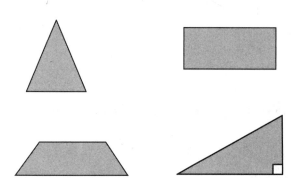

Show What You Know!

Solve each problem. Identify the strategy you used.

1. What is this shape?

_____

2. What is the measure of each angle?

_____

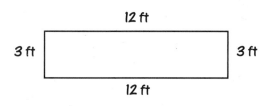

3. What is the area of the rectangle?
(Remember: A = W × H)

_____

4. What is the perimeter of the rectangle?
(Remember: P = 2W + 2H)

_____

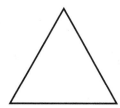

5. What is this shape?

_____

6. What is the measure of each angle?

_____

Unit 9 Review, page 2

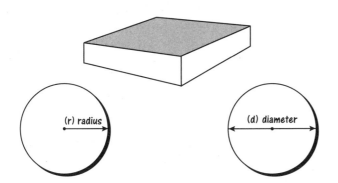

Show What You Know!

Solve each problem. Identify the strategy you used.

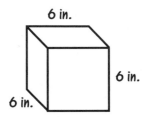

1. What is the total surface area of the cube?

_____

2. What is the volume of the cube?

_____

3. What is the radius of the circle in the next column?

_____

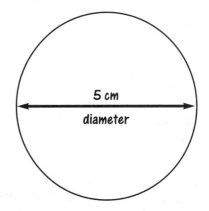

4. What is the circumference of the circle?

_____

5. What is the area of the circle?

_____

Extension...

Measure an object that is a rectangle, such as a bulletin board. What is the area? perimeter? Measure the diameter of a circle, such as the face of a clock. What is the radius? circumference? area? Measure a rectangular box, such as a textbook. What is the length? width? height? total surface area?

Problem Solving Strategies 6, SV 0517-0

Name _____ Date _____

FLEX YOUR MATH MUSCLES

One day Flex decided to do some math problems about shapes and objects.
Help Flex to solve these problems. Use the correct formula from the list below.

To find the area of a rectangle, use the formula $A = W \times H$.
To find the perimeter of a rectangle, use the formula $P = 2W + 2H$.
To find the circumference of a circle, use the formula $C = \pi d$.
To find the area of a circle, use the formula $A = \pi r^2$.
To find the volume of a rectangular box, use the formula $V = W \times L \times H$.

1

Flex had a sheet of plywood in his shop. It was 8 feet long and 4 feet wide. What was the area of the plywood?

_____

2

Flex had a box that was 6 inches high, 10 inches wide, and 12 inches long. He had 750 cubic inches of sawdust to put in the box. Would all the sawdust fit in the box?

_____

3

What was the volume of Flex's box?

_____

4

Flex wanted to put a round pond in his backyard. He had picked out a spot that was 12 feet wide and 12 feet long. He designed a pond with a circumference of 34.54 feet. Would the pond fit in the spot Flex had picked?

_____

5

What was the area of the spot Flex had selected?

_____

6

What was the area of the pond Flex had designed?

_____

BOTH SIDES ARE THE SAME

Strategy: Write an Equation

Most math problems give you all the numbers you need to solve the problem. Some problems do not give all the numbers. These problems have an unknown, also called a variable. We use a letter to represent the variable.

Algebra is a kind of mathematics that uses variables. These variables are part of an equation. An equation is like a formula. In an equation, the values on 1 side of the equal sign are the same as the values on the other side. Because the values are the same, you can solve the equation to find the variable.

STEP 1 **Read the problem.**
Cal has 27 models. Of these, 12 are model ships. The rest are model airplanes. How many airplanes does Cal have?

STEP 2 **Write an equation.**
The unknown number is how many airplanes Cal has. This unknown number, or variable, is usually called x. An equation to find x can be written in 2 ways. One way uses addition: 12 ships + x airplanes = 27 models. A second way uses subtraction: 27 models − 12 ships = x airplanes.

Try It! Write 1 addition and 1 subtraction equation for each problem. You do not have to solve the equations.

1. Cal has 12 model ships. Of these, 5 are aircraft carriers, and the rest are cruisers. How many cruisers does Cal have?

_____

2. Cal also likes to collect coins. He has 38 old coins. Of these, 21 are dimes, and the rest are pennies. How many pennies does Cal have?

_____

3. Cal has 21 dimes in his coin collection. Of these, 16 are Roosevelt dimes, and the rest are Liberty dimes. How many Liberty dimes does Cal have?

_____

4. Cal also collects stamps. He has 43 foreign stamps. Of these, 18 are from England. The rest are from Mexico. How many Mexican stamps does Cal have?

_____

Name _____ Date _____

X MARKS THE SPOT!

Strategy: Write an Equation

Equations can also use multiplication and division. Even though the operations are different, multiplication and division equations are written the same way. You still need to find the variable.

STEP 1 **Read the problem.**
Susan had 20 cookies. She gave an equal number of cookies to each of her 5 friends. How many cookies did Susan give each friend?

STEP 2 **Write an equation.**
The variable is how many cookies Susan gave each friend. The equation to find the variable, x, can be written in 2 ways. One way uses multiplication:
5 friends $\times$ x cookies each = 20 cookies
A second way uses division:
20 cookies $\div$ 5 friends = x cookies each
or 20 cookies $\div$ x cookies each = 5 friends

Try It! Write 1 equation using multiplication and 1 equation using division for each problem. You do not have to solve the equations.

1. Susan made 24 sandwiches for the picnic. She made an equal number of 3 different kinds of sandwiches. How many of each kind did she make?

_____

2. Susan made 24 sandwiches for the picnic. She put an equal amount of sandwiches in 6 sacks. How many sandwiches did Susan put in each sack?

_____

3. Susan bought 36 cans of soda for the picnic. She bought an equal number of cola, root beer, and orange sodas. How many cans of each kind did she buy?

_____

4. Susan brought 28 treats to the picnic. She had an equal amount of cookies, cupcakes, granola bars, and crackers. How many of each kind of treat did she bring?

_____

Problem Solving Strategies 6, SV 0517-0

Name _____ Date _____

WHAT IS X?

Strategy: Write an Equation

When you solve an equation, you must find the value of the unknown number, or variable.

 Read the problem.

Jenny has 22 CDs. That is 5 more than Maria has. How many CDs does Maria have?

 Write an equation.

Let x = the number of CDs Maria has. You can use either addition or subtraction to write the equation.

x CDs Maria has + 5 more = 22 CDs Jenny has

or 22 CDs Jenny has − 5 more = x CDs Maria has

STEP 3 **Solve the equation.**

To solve for x, you must get x alone on 1 side of the equals sign.

$x + 5 = 22$ $\qquad x + 5 - 5 = 22 - 5$ $\qquad x = 17$

or $22 - 5 = x$ $\qquad 17 = x$ $\qquad$ Maria has 17 CDs.

Try It! Write an equation using addition or subtraction for each problem. Then solve each equation. (Hint: Let x = the variable.)

1. Maria has 17 CDs. Of these, 9 are rock music, and the rest are pop music. How many pop music CDs does Maria have?

_____

2. Maria has 17 CDs. This is 14 fewer CDs than her friend Lewann has. How many CDs does Lewann have?

_____

3. Lewann wants to see her favorite band. Tickets cost $15 each. This is $4 more than Lewann has. How much money does Lewann have?

_____

4. Lewann's dad says he will give Lewann the extra money if she will wash dishes 20 days in the next month. This is 3 days more than she already washes the dishes. How many days does Lewann wash the dishes now?

_____

Unit 10, Pre-Algebra
Problem Solving Strategies 6, SV 0517-0

Name _____ Date _____

MORE EQUATIONS TO SOLVE

Strategy: Write an Equation

Equations can also be solved using multiplication and division. Again, you must find the value of the variable.

STEP 1 ⟩ Read the problem.
Jason wants to buy a new video game that costs $30. This is 2 times the amount of money Jason has. How much money does Jason have now?

STEP 2 ⟩ Write an equation.
Let x = the money Jason has now. You can write an equation using either multiplication or division. x money Jason has × 2 times more = $30 cost of game or $30 cost of game ÷ 2 times more = x money Jason has

STEP 3 ⟩ Solve the equation.
You must get x alone on 1 side of the equals sign.
$x \times 2 = \$30$ $x \times \frac{2}{2} = \frac{\$30}{2}$ $x \times 1 = \$15$ $x = \$15$
or $\$30 \div 2 = x$ $\$15 = x$ Jason has $15 now.

Try It! Write an equation using multiplication or division for each problem. Then solve each equation. (Hint: Let x = the variable.)

1. In Jason's video game, he has to solve a problem about a rectangular room before he can leave it. The area of the room is 180 square feet, and it has a width of 15 feet. What is the length of the room? (Remember the formula: Area = length × width.)

_____

2. In another part of the game, Jason is trapped in a circle. To escape he must find the diameter of the circle. The circumference of the circle is 40.82 feet. What is the diameter of the circle? (Remember the formula: Circumference = π × diameter.)

_____

3. Jason must solve a final problem before he can finish the game. The Red Gorp has 72 shots left. This is 3 times as many shots as the Blue Gorp has left. How many shots does the Blue Gorp have left?

_____

4. At the end, Jason has scored 96 points. His score is 3 times better than Kyle's best score. What is Kyle's best score?

_____

Problem Solving Strategies 6, SV 0517-0

Name _____ Date _____

GET TOGETHER!

Strategy: Identify Substeps

You know that in addition and multiplication you don't have to work the problem in any special order. The numbers $4 + 5 + 6$ can also be added as $6 + 5 + 4$, and the sum is the same. The numbers $3 \times 4 \times 5$ can be written as $5 \times 3 \times 4$, and the product is the same.

But when multiple operations are included, order is important. The problem $4 \times 5 + 2$ is not the same as the problem $4 + 2 \times 5$. To keep numbers organized in equations, parentheses are used.

 Read the problem.
$x = 4(5 + 2) - 2(3 - 1)$

 Identify the substeps.

Substep 1: First add and subtract the numbers in the parentheses.
Substep 2: The 4 and 2 beside the parentheses mean to multiply those numbers by the number in the parentheses.
Substep 3: Finally, subtract to find x.

STEP 3 **Work the substeps. Solve the problem.**
$x = 4(5 + 2) - 2(3 - 1)$
$x = 4(7) - 2(2)$ $x = 28 - 4$ $x = 24$

Try It! Write an equation to solve each problem. Be sure to group your functions using parentheses.

1. Kay has 24 trading cards. Kent has twice as many less 4. How many cards does Kent have?

_____

2. In July Kent got 2 paychecks for $85.00 each. He had to pay 3 bills of $50.00 each. How much money did Kent have left?

_____

3. Kay took a test in math. Each correct answer was worth 5 points. Each wrong answer counted off 4 points. Kay had 17 correct answers and 3 wrong answers. What was her final score?

_____

4. At the end of August, Kay had $80.00. Kent had 3 times as much less $15.00. How much money did Kent have at the end of August?

_____

Name _____ Date _____

INTO THE UNKNOWN!

Strategy: Write an Equation

You have learned how to solve equations with a single unknown or variable. But some equations have more than 1 variable. And sometimes the variable has a beginning value greater than x.

STEP 1 ▶ Read the problem.

At the basketball game, floor seats cost $3 each and bleacher seats cost $2 each. Your class buys $70 worth of tickets, with 10 more bleacher seats than floor seats. How many of each type of ticket does the class buy?

STEP 2 ▶ Write an equation.

Let x = floor seats.

$3x + $2(x + 10 more bleacher seats) = $70

STEP 3 ▶ Solve the equation.

First do the arithmetic. $3x + $2(x + 10) = $70

$3x + $2x + $20 = $70

Now get all the variables on 1 side of the equals sign and all the known numbers on the other side. Remember to change signs when you move from 1 side of the equals sign to the other side.

$5x + $20 − $20 = $70 − $20 $5x = $50 $x = \dfrac{\$50}{\$5}$ $x = 10$

Your class buys 10 floor seats and 20 bleacher seats.

Try It!   Write an equation for each problem. Then solve the equation.

1. Find this number. This number added to 4 times this number equals 15. Call this number x. What is the value of x?

_____

2. Here's another number to find. The value of 3 times this number minus 6 equals 2 times this number plus 6. Call this number x. What is the value of x?

_____

3. Mr. Allen took his family to the movies. Tickets were $7 for adults and $4 for children. He gave the clerk $30 and received $8 in change. How many of each ticket did Mr. Allen buy?

_____

Unit 10, Pre-Algebra
Problem Solving Strategies 6, SV 0517-0

Name _____ Date _____

MORE OR LESS?

Strategy: Use an Inequality

Sometimes equations are not equal. These unequal equations are called inequalities. Inequalities do not use the equal sign. Instead, they use the "greater than" sign ($>$) and the "less than" sign ($<$). Hint: the point of these signs always aims at the smaller number.

STEP 1 Read the problem.
Together Sandra and Nadene have less than 20 movie posters. Sandra has 4 more posters than Nadene. How many posters might Nadene have?

STEP 2 Write an inequality.
Let x = Nadene's posters.
$x + (x + 4) < 20$

STEP 3 Solve the inequality.
$x + (x + 4) < 20$
$2x + 4 < 20$ $2x < 20 - 4$ $\frac{2x}{2} < \frac{16}{2}$ $x < 8$
Nadene has fewer than 8 posters.

Try It! Write an inequality and then solve each problem.

1. The value of x plus 3 is greater than 12. What might the value of x be?

_____

2. Ten times the value of x plus 7 is less than 47. What is the value of x?

_____

3. Together Nick and Raul scored more than 40 points in a basketball game. Nick scored 6 more points than Raul. How many points might Raul have scored? (Hint: Let x = Raul's score.)

_____

4. Carol and Conrad together have less than $50. Carol has $10 more than Conrad. How much money might Conrad have? (Hint: Let x = Conrad's money.)

_____

5. How much money might Carol have?

_____

Problem Solving Strategies 6, SV 0517-0

Unit 10 Review

Strategies
- Write an Equation
- Identify Substeps
- Use an Inequality

Show What You Know!

Solve each problem. Identify the strategy you used.

1. Gene drew 15 pictures of dinosaurs. Of these, 6 were meat-eaters. The rest were plant-eaters. How many plant-eaters did Gene draw?

_____

2. Selena jogged 2 miles on Monday, Wednesday, and Friday. For the week, she jogged a total of 8 miles. If she jogged the same number of miles on Tuesday and Thursday, how many miles did she jog on each of those days?

_____

3. Together Pete and William earned less than $50 doing chores for their neighbors. If Pete earned at least $20, how much money might William have earned?

_____

4. Gregor is 12 years old. His brother is 7 years older. What equation could you use to figure out how old Gregor's brother is?

_____

5. A scientist has traveled to 26 different countries. Of these, 19 are located in the Western Hemisphere. The rest are located in the Eastern Hemisphere. How many countries did the scientist travel to in the Eastern Hemisphere?

_____

Name _____ Date _____

Unit 10 Review, page 2

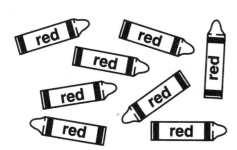

Strategies
- Write an Equation
- Identify Substeps
- Use an Inequality

Show What You Know!

1. The kindergarten teacher had 36 crayons. There were 4 children at the art table. The teacher gave each child the same number of crayons. How many crayons did each child get?

_____

2. Remi has 27 books on her bookshelf in her bedroom. Of these, 10 or fewer of them are mysteries. How many books are probably not mysteries?

_____

Solve each problem. Identify the strategy you used.

3. A school had a total of 21 classrooms for grades 6, 7, and 8. Every year, at least 7 of those classrooms are used by sixth-graders. How many classrooms are probably used by seventh- and eighth-graders?

_____

4. A dealership had 50 cars on display. There were 5 rows of cars. There was an equal number of cars in each row. How many cars were in each row?

_____

Extension..

Look at a biography of a famous person in history, such as George Washington Carver. Use the following equation to find out how old the person was when he or she died. Let x stand for the person's age.

Year of birth $+ x =$ Year of death

Name _____ Date _____

FLEX YOUR MATH MUSCLES

One evening Flex was sitting by his backyard pond. He was thinking about all the math he had learned recently. Help Flex review by solving these problems.

1

Flex was planning to build a square shed in his backyard. If the floor size was 8 feet by 8 feet, what would be the total area of the floor?

_____

3

Flex looked at the sky. The weather report had predicted a 25% chance of rain. What was the probability it would rain?

_____

2

Flex was going to add a round window to his shop. The window would have a circumference of 43.96 inches. What would be the radius of the window?

_____

4

Flex had 2 final projects to build. He knew that one project would use 2 times as many nails as the other. He had 120 nails. How many nails could he use in each project?

_____

Problem Solving Strategies 6, SV 0517-0

Answer Key

Assessment
Page 6
1. 2,000 spangles
2. no
3. Megan won.
4. yes
5. 2-1/8 pages
6. 4-1/3 laps

Page 7
7. 3/8
8. 1-1/4 ounces
9. 21 smaller servings. He used 3-3/4 cups of gravy in his goulash.
10. 0.67575 pounds
11. 3 pitchers
12. $5.00
13. yes

Page 8
14. 18 feet
15. 11 in 30 or 11/30
16. 0.250
17. 103.62 square inches
18. 64 cubic inches
19. Equations will vary. Maria has 8 pop music CDs.
20. Raul scored more than 17 points.

Whole Numbers
Page 9
1. 2,000 spangles
2. 7 pages
3. 800 miles
4. 1,600 miles

Page 10
1. 13 decorations
2. 52 free tickets
3. 32,376 kernels
4. 9 pairs

Page 11
1. 6 hours
2. yes
3. no
4. $19.00

Page 12
1. $675 \times 33 \div 75 = 297$
2. $210 \times 3 - 321 + 4 = 313$
3. $195 + 3 \times 4 \div 24 - 5 = 28$

Page 13
1. 7,285 people vanished
2. 3,760 people remained
3. no
4. 21 postcards

Page 15
1. Miami
2. Austin
3. 11,000 T-shirts
4. 22,000 T-shirts
5. $33,000.00
6. $66,000.00
7. $242,000.00

Page 16
1. 90; Identify Substeps
2. $224 \div 2 - 12 \times 3 = 300$; Choose an Operation
3. 41; Work Backward
4. $224; Identify Substeps
5. 460; Use Estimation

Page 17
1. Tussi Orchard
2. Smith Orchard
3. 700 bushels
4. 1,600 bushels
5. $1,000
6. $1,500
7. $8,000

Page 18
1. 0
2. Possible answers. Some answers may vary.
   a. $2 \div 2 \times 2 \div 2 = 1$
   b. $2 - 2 \times 2 + 2 = 2$
   c. $2 \times 2 + 2 \div 2 = 3$
   d. $2 \times 2 \times 2 \div 2 = 4$
   e. $2 \div 2 + 2 + 2 = 5$
   f. $2 \times 2 \times 2 - 2 = 6$
3. Possible answers. Some answers may vary.
   a. $3 + 3 + 3 \div 3 = 3$
   b. $3 \times 3 + 3 \div 3 = 4$
   c. $3 + 3 \div 3 + 3 = 5$
   d. $3 + 3 \times 3 \div 3 = 6$
   e. $3 \div 3 + 3 + 3 = 7$

Fractions
Page 19
1. 4 shirts
2. 4/16 or 1/4
3. 2 dresses
4. 2/10 or 1/5

Page 20
1. 1/6 more dinosaur toys
2. 4/7 were yo-yos.
3. 8/12 or 2/3
4. 4/12 or 1/3

Page 21
1. Megan won.
2. Jimmy
3. Mary won.
4. Katie won.

Page 22
1. bottoms
2. 8/9 of a roll
3. 1/9 of a roll
4. 5/8 of the bows were used.
5. 3/8 of the bows were left.
6. 3/7 had gold ribbon.

Page 23
1. 2/12 or 1/6 of a sheet
2. yes
3. 11/12 of a bag
4. 1/12 of a bag left

Page 25
1. 46 feet of wood
2. 10-foot counter and 4-foot counter
3. 154 feet
4. 90/154 or 45/77
5. 48/154 or 24/77
6. 16/154 or 8/77
7. two 8-foot counters and one 4-foot counter
8. 8-foot counters = 48/64 or 3/4; 4-foot counter = 16/64 or 1/4

Page 26
1. 1/10; Use a Drawing
2. Yuki; Use Equivalent Fractions
3. 1-1/4 hour; Choose an Operation
4. 4/35; Use Equivalent Fractions, Choose an Operation, Identify Substeps
5. 3/5; Choose an Operation, Identify Substeps

Page 27
1. 3/10
2. 1/2
3. 1/2
4. 67/70
5. 3/70
6. No, she only has 3 yards of material left and the smallest costume requires 4 yards.

Page 28
1. 1/4 of a pie
2. none
3. Flex: $10,000.00; brother: $6,000.00; sister: $4,000.00
4. yes
5. 5/6 of a yard for $4.50

Improper Fractions
Page 29
1. Both are same size.
2. Tuesday
3. Both worried same amount.
4. Tanisha

Page 30
1. no
2. 33/4 liters or 8-1/4 liters

Page 31
1. second day
2. 17/8 or 2-1/8 pages
3. Planet Z was closer.
4. 1/15 light-year

Page 32
1. Second landing spot was closer.
2. 1/8 space-mile
3. 4-5/12 liters
4. Second tank held more.
5. 2-9/10 units
6. 37-1/10 units

Page 33
1. Tanisha
2. 1/8 pound more
3. 13/16 pound

4. 7-4/10 or 7-2/5 hours
5. 2-4/10 or 2-2/5 hours longer

Pages 34—35
Magic Gates are:
C, E, F, G, N, R, S.
A. 1/2
B. 5/12
C. 3-7/13
D. 9-5/9
E. 1/4
F. 1-1/2
G. 9/16
H. 10
I. 3/4
J. 2-1/2
K. 1/10
L. 15-5/28
M. 7/8
N. 1-1/3
O. 7/9
P. 1
Q. 2-1/20
R. 10-7/12
S. 4-3/16
T. 3-7/12

Page 36
1. 1-3/7; Make a Model
2. 1-1/8 + 19/16 + 5/4 = 18/16 + 19/16 + 20/16 = 57/16 = 3-9/16; Write a Number Sentence
3. 11-9/12; Identify Substeps
4. 3-3/8 = 27/8; 3-1/2 = 28/8; Jeremy used more ribbon.; 28/8 − 27/8 = 1/8 feet; Jeremy used 1/8 feet more ribbon than Mary.; Choose an Operation
5. Quinn should use nails that are 2-1/2 inches long so it goes through 2-3/8 inches, the combined thickness of the boards.; Use Logical Reasoning

Page 37
1. 4-3/4 + 2-1/4 = 7; Write a Number Sentence
2. The 2 circles would be 6/3, but 7 flowers would need 7/3. Therefore, Mrs. Anderson does not have enough circles to

make 7 flowers.; Use Logical Reasoning
3. 2-5/12 hours; Choose an Operation, Identify Substeps
4. 7-3/8; Choose an Operation, Identify Substeps

Page 38
1. 2-3/5 boxes
2. country: 25; rock: 40; hip-hop: 35
3. 4-11/12 cans
4. 8-5/12 feet

Multiplying Fractions
Page 39
1. 4 arrows
2. 32 free throws
3. 60 strikes
4. 40 balls

Page 40
1. 4/15 of the mail
2. 44 letters
3. 97 letters
4. 70 magazines donated
5. 42 magazines used for scrapbooks
6. 28 magazines left

Page 41
1. 7/16 cup bleach
2. 1/4 cup pepper
3. 6 cups broth
4. 39

Page 42
1. 1-2/5 miles
2. 4-1/3 laps

Page 43
1. 3/8
2. 5/8
3. other kinds of pizza
4. 5-1/8 pounds

Page 44
1. 6-1/4 cups water
2. 2-1/3 teaspoons

Page 45
1. 24 seconds
2. 210 seconds
3. 1-1/6 minutes faster

Page 46
1. 22 points; Choose an Operation
2. 1/12 pound; Write a Number Sentence
3. 3; Choose an Operation

4. 3/4 hour; Guess and Check, Choose an Operation, Write a Number Sentence
5. 4-3/8; Identify Substeps

Page 47
1. 7/10
2. 3/10
3. 2-3/5 cups
4. 3-1/4 cups
5. No, the fractions shown in the model tell how much of the recipe is rolled oats, dried fruit, and assorted nuts, regardless of how much granola he makes. However, the actual amounts he uses to make the recipe will be 1/2 of the original amounts.

Page 48
1. 1/2
2. 4
3. 25
4. 48
5. 24
6. 12
7. 6
8. 2/3
9. 2/3
10. 1,234
11. 1,234
12. 1,234

Dividing Fractions
Page 49
1. 384 salespeople
2. 24 badges
3. 20 quarters

Page 51
1. 2/9 of the files
2. 1/4 dozen
3. 3 doughnuts
4. 1/4 pizza
5. 1/6 of a gallon
6. 5/24
7. 5 pieces
8. 1/3 dozen cookies

Page 52
1. 1-1/4 ounces
2. 1-5/6 dozen
3. 22 flowers
4. 4/5 sheet

Page 53
1. 38 smaller meatballs. He bought 2 pounds of beef.
2. 30 slices. She used 1/2 cup of nuts and 3/4 cup of honey in the recipe.

Page 54
1. 15 casts
2. 8 bandages
3. 6 days
4. 26 packages

Page 55
1. Ruben: 5/6 ÷ 1/5 = 5/6 × 5/1 = 25/6 = 4-1/6
   Milly: 4/6 ÷ 1/5 = 4/6 × 5/1 = 20/6 = 3-2/6 or 3-1/3
   Chan: 3/6 ÷ 1/5 = 3/6 × 5/1 = 15/6 = 2-3/6 or 2-1/2
   Rosa: 2/6 ÷ 1/5 = 2/6 × 5/1 = 10/6 = 1-4/6 or 1-2/3
   Skip: 1/6 ÷ 1/5 = 1/6 × 5/1 = 5/6 = 5/6

Page 56
1. 1/4 pound; Write a Number Sentence, Choose an Operation
2. 1-5/8 feet; Identify Extra Information
3. 1/4; Write a Number Sentence, Choose an Operation
4. 1/5; Make a Model
5. 1/10; Make a Model
6. 7/24; Write a Number Sentence, Choose an Operation

Page 57
1. 40/12; 3-1/3; Look for a Pattern
2. 48/12; 4; Look for a Pattern
3. 56/12; 4-2/3; Look for a Pattern
4. 64/12; 5-1/3; Look for a Pattern

Page 58
1. $555.75
2. 15-11/12 pounds
3. 3-1/2 pounds
4. 3/4

Decimals

Page 59
1. $12,000.00
2. $200.00
3. $50.00
4. 35 hours

Page 60
1. $6.84
2. 63 hours
3. 2,500 announcements
4. $19.25

Page 61
1. 28.5 ounces
2. 8 ounces
3. 2.5 ounces
4. 0.5 cup flour; 3 ounces milk; 2 ounces berries

Page 62
1. 5.25 boxes
2. 3.75 boxes
3. 7.2 feet
4. $2.16

Page 63
1. 0.125 ton
2. 0.155 pound
3. 0.67575 pound
4. 53.865 gallons

Page 64
1. 38 slices
2. melons for $0.15 per pound

Page 65
1. 3 pitchers
2. 1.1 ounces
3. $24.65
4. 8 friends

Page 66
1. $35.00; Look for a Pattern
2. $350.00; Look for a Pattern
3. 50.4 miles; Write a Number Sentence
4. $150.00; Look for a Pattern
5. 125; Choose an Operation
6. $23.40; Look for a Pattern
7. 6°; Choose an Operation

Page 67
1. 46.8 pounds; Identify Substeps
2. 5.6 inches; Look for a Pattern

3. He charged $22.50 for each lawn he cut on Monday and $18.75 for each lawn he cut on Tuesday.; Identify Substeps
4. $27.50; Choose an Operation; Identify Substeps
5. 3.72 ounces; Write a Number Sentence

Page 68
1. 77.5 miles
2. 387.5 miles
3. 75 pounds
4. 300 ounces
5. 2.25 pounds
6. $99.75

Ratios and Percentages

Page 69
1. 1 to 2, 1:2, 1/2
2. 1 to 5, 1:5, 1/5
3. 3 to 2, 3:2, 3/2
4. 3 to 5, 3:5, 3/5

Page 70
1. yes
2. no
3. yes
4. no

Page 71
1. $5.00
2. $3.50
3. $2.50
4. $66.00
5. $88.00
6. $11.00

Page 72
1. $4.00
2. $0.08
3. $0.48
4. 2.5 quarts
5. 45 minutes
6. $12.00
7. 5 comic books

Page 73
1. 18 feet
2. 30 feet
3. 28 meters
4. yes

Page 74
1. 70%
2. 30%
3. 16%
4. 84%
5. 75%

6. 25%

Page 75
1. $33.07
2. $10.81
3. $0.62 or $0.63
4. 1,950 nonfiction books
5. 1,050 fiction books

Page 76
1.

10 newspapers	$5.00
20 newspapers	$10.00
30 newspapers	$15.00
40 newspapers	$20.00

Make a Table
2. Yes, the ratios are equal. 16/20 = 4/5; 8/10 = 4/5; 4/5 = 4/5; Set Up a Proportion
3. 9; Set Up a Proportion
4. 3/8; Model a Ratio
5. 1/2; Model a Ratio

Page 77
1. 8/1 = s/12; Set Up a Proportion
2. 35%; Define Percent
3. 40%; Define Percent
4. 25%; Define Percent
5. 5/3 = g/27; Set Up a Proportion
6. 2.54 inches; Identify Substeps

Page 78
1. 18 bean plants
2. 8 to 5, 8:5, 8/5
3. 5 to 8, 5:8, 5/8
4. 75%
5. 8%
6. $2.57

Probability

Page 79
1. 1 in 6 or 1/6
2. 3 in 6 or 1 in 2, 3/6 or 1/2
3. 3 in 6 or 1 in 2, 3/6 or 1/2
4. 5 in 6 or 5/6

Page 80
1. 3 in 10 or 3/10
2. 2 in 10 or 1 in 5, 2/10 or 1/5
3. 6 in 10 or 3 in 5, 6/10 or 3/5
4. 2 in 5 or 2/5

Page 81
1. blue

2. black
3. 5 in 30 or 1 in 6, 5/30 or 1/6
4. 6 in 30 or 1 in 5, 6/30 or 1/5
5. 11 in 30 or 11/30
6. 22 in 30 or 11 in 15, 22/30 or 11/15
7. 10 in 30 or 1 in 3, 10/30 or 1/3
8. 23 in 30 or 23/30

Page 82
1. 20 in 50 or 2 in 5, 20/50 or 2/5
2. 6 in 50 or 3 in 25, 6/50 or 3/25
3. 26 in 50 or 13 in 25, 26/50 or 13/25
4. 5 in 50 or 1 in 10, 5/50 or 1/10
5. 49 in 50 or 49/50
6. 27 in 50 or 27/50
7. 5 in 50 or 1 in 10, 5/50 or 1/10
8. 7 in 50 or 7/50

Page 83
1. 40
2. 52
3. 72
4. 98
5. 180
6. 28

Page 84
1. 0.250
2. 0.333
3. 0.667
4. 0.583
5. 0.428 or 0.429

Page 85
1. 35
2. 60
3. 15
4. 200

Page 86
1. 2/11; Use a Drawing
2. b/100 = 3/10; Set Up a Proportion
3. 4 first-place ribbons ÷ 10 shows = 0.4 first-place average; Write a Number Sentence
4. 60; Use a Table
5. 20; Use a Table

Page 87
1. 0/10
2. 2/10
3. 7/10
4. 3/10

5. 1/7
6. 4/7

Page 88
1. 1 in 2 or 1/2
2. 1 in 2 or 1/2
3. 1 in 6 or 1/6; 5 in 6 or 5/6
4. 0.620
5. 24 games
6. 0.390; 0.610

Geometry
Page 89
1a. equilateral
1b. isosceles
1c. scalene
1d. right
1e. obtuse
2. 60
3. 90
4. less
5. Answers will vary.

Page 90
1a. square
1b. rectangle
1c. parallelogram
1d. trapezoid
2. A, C
3. 180
4. A, C
5. B, D
6. Answers will vary.

Page 91
1. $A = 54$ square feet; $P = 30$ feet
2. $A = 36$ square feet; $P = 24$ feet
3. $A = 24.5$ square feet; $P = 29$ feet
4. Answers will vary.

Page 93
1. 9 inches
2. 43.96 inches
3. 78.5 square inches
4. 3.925 inches
5. 37.68 inches
6. 200.96 square inches
7. 103.62 square inches
8. 30 inches
9. The pond with the circumference of 8 feet has the larger area.

Page 94
1. 304 square inches
2. 150 square inches

Page 95
1. 64 cubic inches
2. 420 cubic inches
3. 343 cubic inches
4. 960 cubic feet

Page 96
1. square; Use a Drawing
2. 90 degrees; Use a Drawing
3. $A = 36$ square feet; Use a Formula
4. $P = 30$ feet; Use a Formula
5. equilateral triangle; Use a Drawing
6. 60 degrees; Use a Drawing

Page 97
1. 216 square inches; Identify Substeps, Use a Drawing, Use a Formula
2. 216 cubic inches; Identify Substeps, Use a Drawing, Use a Formula
3. 2.5 centimeters; Use a Drawing, Use a Formula
4. 15.7 centimeters; Use a Drawing, Use a Formula
5. 19.625 square centimeters; Identify Substeps, Use a Drawing, Use a Formula

Page 98
1. 32 square feet
2. no
3. 720 cubic inches
4. yes
5. 144 square feet
6. 94.985 square feet

Pre-Algebra
Page 99
Possible answers.
Equations may vary.
1. $5 + x = 12$; $12 - x = 5$
2. $21 + x = 38$; $38 - x = 21$
3. $16 + x = 21$; $21 - x = 16$
4. $18 + x = 43$; $43 - x = 18$

Page 100
Possible answers.
Equations may vary.
1. $3 \times x = 24$; $24 \div x = 3$
2. $6 \times x = 24$; $24 \div x = 6$
3. $3 \times x = 36$; $36 \div x = 3$
4. $4 \times x = 28$; $28 \div x = 4$

Page 101
Equations will vary.
1. Maria has 8 pop music CDs.
2. Lewann has 31 CDs.
3. Lewann has $11.00.
4. Lewann washes dishes 17 times a month now.

Page 102
Equations will vary.
1. The length is 12 feet.
2. The diameter is 13 feet.
3. Blue Gorp has 24 shots left.
4. Kyle's best score is 32.

Page 103
Equations will vary.
1. Kent has 44 cards.
2. Kent has $20.00 left.
3. Kay's final score was 73.
4. Kent had $225.00.

Page 104
1. $x = 3$
2. $x = 12$
3. 2 adult and 2 children tickets

Page 105
1. $x > 9$
2. $x < 4$
3. Raul scored more than 17 points.
4. Conrad had less than $20.00.
5. Carol had less than $30.00.

Page 106
1. 9; Write an Equation
2. 1 mile; Identify Substeps
3. $30 or less; Use an Inequality
4. $12 + 7 = b$ OR $b - 7 = 12$ OR $b - 12 = 7$; Write an Equation
5. 7; Write an Equation

Page 107
1. 9; Write an Equation
2. 17 or more; Use an Inequality
3. 14 or fewer; Use an Inequality
4. 10; Write an Equation

Page 108
1. 64 square feet
2. 7 inches
3. 1 in 4 or 1/4
4. 80 nails and 40 nails